THE MOM IN ME 2

Stories and Practical Advice from Moms Who have Survived Parenting

VISIONARY AUTHOR
KIMMOLY K. LABOO

©Copyright 2021 Kimmoly K. LaBoo

All rights reserved. This book is protected under the copyright laws of the United States of America.

ISBN-13: 978-1-954609-06-8

Library of Congress Control Number: 2020918964

No portion of this book may be reproduced, distributed, or transmitted in any form, including photocopying, recording, or other electronic or mechanical methods, without the written permission of the publisher, except in the case of brief quotations embodied in reviews and certain other non-commercial uses permitted by copyright law. Permission granted on request.

For information regarding special discounts for bulk purchases contact the Publisher:
LaBoo Publishing Enterprise, LLC
staff@laboopublishing.com
www.laboopublishing.com

All information is solely considered as the point of view of the authors.

The Holy Bible, King James Version. Cambridge Edition: 1769; King James Bible Online, 2019. www.kingjamesbibleonline.org.

Scripture taken from the New King James Version®. Copyright © 1982 by Thomas Nelson. Used by permission. All rights reserved.

TABLE OF CONTENTS

Introduction 1

I Was Never Alone – Portia Mosby 3

Just A Conversation With God – Lisa Stokes 15

Enough of the Church – Larvetricus Harris 27

Tomorrow Will Be Better – Jackie Powers 39

Purpose of a Dream – Angela Middleton-Cornish 51

Single Mommy"Ing" It – Latia Reynolds 65

You're Not My Mom – Tamika Decatur 77

Parenting with Bipolar Disorder – Danielle M. Batiste 87

Throwing the Baby Out with the Bath Water –
    Reimagining Rest – Lashonda Durden 97

About the Visionary Author 111

Also by Kimmoly K. Laboo 113

INTRODUCTION

As a mom of two grown sons, I often look back at the decisions I've made throughout their lives, wondering if I got it right. Are there things I could have or should have done differently? The answer, of course, is that the choices I made directly impacted who they are as young men today. I see my choices reflected in who they are daily. While there are things I wish I could have a do-over with, I've learned to extend myself grace. I know that I did the best I could while I was raising them. I missed the mark in many ways, but I fared pretty well in other areas.

When I look at my sons now, I am grateful for the privilege of being their mom. I not only love them, I like them, and I believe the feeling is mutual. Even as our children grow into adults, we never stop being a mom.

Being a mom is a wonderful gift, one that will challenge and grow you in the most beautiful ways. I raise my hat, heels, and lashes to moms everywhere. Stay the course, enjoy the journey, extend yourself grace and watch your baby grow with love and admiration. Know you are doing the best you can, even when it feels like you're not.

Stay Amazing,

Kimmoly K. LaBoo

Portia Mosby is a loving, single mother of three adult children and a Mimi of two beautiful grands. Originally from Pennsylvania, she relocated to Grand Rapids, Michigan in 2017 in pursuit of a fresh start. She is known for encouraging others, powerful prayers, her bold faith in Jesus Christ, and her strength.

She has served in the healthcare field for over ten years. Her love, deep passion for people and the desire to care for them has made an incredible impact on those she's helped. She's had humbling opportunities to partner with women and children's shelters, food pantries and has helped the homeless in her home state. Her ministry work will continue with evangelizing and sharing her testimony during mission trips.

When she is not working full-time, she enjoys spending time with God and her family. Portia is preparing to get into the travel industry following the launch her first, highly anticipated published book, "My Scars Tell A Story". She is currently an Amazon Best-Selling author of a book anthology project called, "The Day She Left Survivor's Diary" and was presented with the opportunity to be interviewed by her local television station to talk about her chapter, which aired during Sexual Assault Awareness Month.

I WAS NEVER ALONE
PORTIA MOSBY

I was 15 and remember being taken to this building downtown in the city where I lived. I was scared, anxious and felt alone. When I entered the building, it was dark and cold. I was asking myself if I should really be there because something in me was screaming this was all wrong. Employees were staring at me, which made me even more uncomfortable and scared. I wanted to turn around and walk out the door, but I didn't. I don't know why. I didn't know what to expect or even what to say. I walked up to the front counter and told them who I was, checked in and then sat and filled out some paperwork while waiting to be called on. Finally, the lady at the front desk called my name and I was escorted through a door, down a long, dark hall, and led to a room. I felt like I was in a creepy movie. When I walked into the room, I saw all sorts of instruments and my eyes felt like they were about to pop out of their sockets. I grew more terrified, wondering what they were for. The room was dark and cold too. I wanted to leave badly but again, I didn't. I was too terrified to move.

I waited in the room for at least ten minutes and then the door opened. A doctor came in with a nurse and explained what was going to happen and what would follow. I was told to remove all my clothing and then put on a gown that was lying on the table.

The doctor made me feel like he was not interested in me or the mental space I was in. The message I received from him was that he wanted to just do his job and leave. No questions. No compassion. No emotion. No conversation. Nothing. The nurse who aided him was very compassionate and held my hand. She talked to me and told me that I had a choice. I could change my mind and leave. I didn't have to go through with the procedure. She was the only person who told me I had a choice. My mind was racing; I was paralyzed with fear, very confused and conflicted. I didn't fully understand what was happening or why I was made to feel that I didn't have a say in the decision that was clearly made for me. After thirty minutes or so, it was done. My pregnancy was ended. I'd just had an abortion at 15 years old.

Shortly after, I was taken to an open recovery room with several empty beds and given a plastic bag with personal hygiene items inside, along with instructions. I felt worse than I did before I walked in the building. I was filled with hurt, disgust, shame, guilt, remorse and regret. I knew in my heart that I should've left. I was an emotional wreck. I felt horrible. I had so many questions, like what it would have been like to be a mom at such a youthful age. Some would say that I was just a baby myself. I was an immature and scared 15-year-old who couldn't even take care of herself, let alone a child. My boyfriend at the time, the baby's father, was also young and scared.

If I knew then what I know now and had an opportunity to go back and change things, I would. If it had been completely left up to me to decide, I would've had my baby and faced all the challenges. Instead, I was left with the emotional and mental scars to deal with, until I wasn't. This just added to all the other trauma and pain I had already been suffering. How would I live with this? I just knew God was angry and disappointed with me and that is what ate at me for years. Would He forgive me? This was the question I always asked myself. Later in my journey throughout motherhood, I was reminded of God's word. **I acknowledged my sin to you, and my iniquity I have not hidden. I said, "I will confess my transgressions to the Lord, and you forgave the iniquity of my sin." Proverbs 32:5, NKJV**

When We Know Better, We Do Better
~Maya Angelou

It had been seven years since the abortion. I was 21 years old and discovered I was pregnant. It was like I was pregnant for the first time and God was giving me a clean slate. I was so happy and excited! He had given me a second chance and I wasn't going to disappoint Him. There was an urgency and obligation to please Him and make Him proud. My child's father was a few years younger than me, and he was very scared. He wasn't ready to be a dad and it would become clear when my daughter was born. I had a great pregnancy and my daughter's father was there for it all. I enjoyed watching and feeling her grow inside me and experiencing the ups and downs of carrying a child. There is absolutely nothing in the world like carrying a child and giving birth. It's so beautiful. I was amazed by what the female body could do and how we could endure all the physical changes and challenges. I would think to myself, wow, there is no other human being in existence that can carry another life inside of them but a woman. After I had my daughter, I appreciated that even more. Giving birth is a beautiful display of love. I told myself repeatedly that I would be the best mom to my baby girl. I never felt love like this before. She made me see myself as if I had a superpower. At the time it was silly but also realistic. It was different and powerful. I went on to have two more beautiful babies, a boy and then another girl. My first daughter and my son have the same father but my baby girl has a different father. I had so many challenges with both fathers, but I did the best I could. I never imagined being a single mom, let alone not coparenting with either of them. It was difficult but there was nothing left to do but keep going. My babies have always made parenting and motherhood worthwhile.

> **For I know the plans that I think toward you, says the Lord, thoughts of peace and not of evil, to give you a future and a hope. Jeremiah 29:11, NKJV**

There are so many levels to parenting. It doesn't matter if you are a single parent, coparenting or both parents are involved, in a relationship, and living in the same household. I learned quickly that I would never be the perfect parent and that I would make many mistakes. Being a single mom doesn't come with a handbook. There is no right or wrong way to parent. It's just your own unique way. As I learned the personalities of each of my babies, it taught me how to deal with them as individuals. I often laughed because I would always think of them as little people when they were toddlers and even going into elementary school. I also learned that just because I was a single mom did not mean I would not go through my own personal struggles. I raised my first child and my second like they were twins. It was so hard, but I did it. They are 10 months apart. So they are always the same age for two months.

Their father wasn't always around the way he should've been. He had struggles of his own that he was dealing with. Some were the result of bad choices and some were because life just happened. He was tall, dark, handsome and very smart but had experienced some very traumatic events at an early age. He was in and out of jail for most of their lives. He was also very misguided, in my opinion. Our relationship only lasted a few years and then we decided to go our separate ways. We came from two completely different backgrounds and were young trying to just really discover who we were. As I mentioned earlier, he wasn't ready to be a dad.

I got pregnant with my youngest child when I was 28 years old and had her when I was 29. She is my miracle baby. When I had my son at 23, I signed paperwork for the delivering doctor to do a procedure and tie my tubes. He was of African descent and tried to convince me that I needed more children because I wasn't married yet. I guess he thought he knew what was best for me. I was adamant about not wanting any more children. In my mind at that time, I had my daughter and my son, and it was a real struggle with just them. I was devastated when I found out that I was pregnant with my baby girl because I thought my tubes were tied and I was done having children. I found out that the doctor who delivered my son did not do the procedure I had signed a legal document for. He only put some sort of clamps on the ends of my tubes that would prevent pregnancy for up to five years and then they would fall off and dissolve. He never said anything to me about what he'd done afterwards. I thought about suing him but then my baby girl was born, and she changed everything! My son and baby girl are six years apart. God always knows exactly what and who we need, and His timing is impeccable.

My baby girl's dad was Jamaican. I met him in a reggae club while in Philadelphia, PA. He was controlling, ignorant and believed that women should only be seen and not heard. Our relationship did not last long. He came across a young woman who would never be submissive to anyone other than her husband. She was me. He didn't like when I would stand up for myself and not do what he wanted me to do. He knew that he couldn't control me. So, that ended quickly.

When I discovered that I was pregnant, I called and told him and in typical deadbeat fashion, he said my baby girl wasn't his. I completely lost it and stopped communicating with him until after she was born. I went to the courthouse and filed a petition for a DNA test and who would've known—the results came back that he was the father of my baby girl. There was no way he could deny her. I remember being in Philly in the elevator of the courthouse with both. She was just 10 months old. He had nothing to say to either of us. It was complete silence. It was the very first time he'd ever seen her, and it was the last. Over the course of her life, he only paid child support because he was forced to. He tried to manipulate me a few times into closing his case by telling me he wanted to meet her, be a father to her and rekindle whatever it was that we had. I never fell for it because if that was the case, he would've done that from the beginning. It was his choice not to be active in her life. The pain and trauma it caused my baby girl was life-changing for her.

It was the same for my oldest daughter and son. The only difference is that they knew who their father was and he was there in the beginning, but baby girl had never even met her father at an age where she would remember who he was. The heartbreak and trauma my babies were burdened with by having absent fathers shaped who they are. The challenges they faced mentally, emotionally, physically and spiritually were heartbreaking. To be present and see the trauma and pain they all had to endure because of someone else's choices was traumatic for me. There is so much pain and anguish in seeing your children suffer and feeling like there is nothing you can do to help them. That crushed me. It hurt my soul. What made it more difficult for all of us is that I was dealing with my own personal trauma and pain. It was so much to deal with and at times, I didn't know how I was going to even come through for them. I couldn't handle my own mess. I didn't have the mental space or strength. We were all in very dark places. My babies were watching and paying close attention to how I would handle things. It was imperative that I get it right, but it didn't always happen that way. None of us ever had our fathers consistently in our lives. This was generational and decisions had to be made if we wanted to get pass the trauma and transition into healthy places in our lives. This too would pass.

I grew up in church and I am a pastor's kid. My family and I were all taught to love the Lord. We are true believers of Jesus Christ, but we are far from perfect. There is this misconception that believers are supposed to be without sin. That's not true. I also raised my babies to be believers in Jesus Christ. They all know who He is and have their own personal relationships with Him. I've always tried to be the best person and mom I could be for my babies. I'd always carried the weight of being both mom and dad to all of them. I'd always felt like I had to do it alone even when God sent help my way through family, friends and strangers. I know this may sound clichéd, but it really does take a village to raise a child. I was often reminded that asking for help didn't mean I was a failure. I learned that throughout my journey of motherhood. As a believer in Christ, I am confident that He will never waste the pain that we face in this life. He will turn it all around to work for our good. I was reminded that there would always be trouble in this world and to expect it, but God has overcome it all. He's victorious and so are those who believe in Him. I believe unless we experience hardship and suffering, we can't truly help someone else that may be dealing with difficulties and pain. It's only through our own sufferings that we can fully understand what others walk through. God will always use what we've experienced to help someone else. The darkest places in our lives and the victories that come from those dark places may lead others to their victories.

Being a single mom, I've had some good days and some not so much. The good ones definitely outweighed the bad ones. My babies are all adults now, but they will always be my babies. My oldest daughter is 27, my son is 26 and my baby girl is 20. With all they have endured, they still have their struggles in certain areas of their lives, but they have overcome so much and are working hard toward their healing and freedom from their emotional and mental prisons. Their dads may not have been a positive or active presence in their lives, but they know they've always had a Heavenly Father who is a consistent presence for them. He has been a Father of the fatherless. He stepped in and did what their dads could not do. Now they are learning to rely on Him. They have turned out to be some pretty amazing human beings and I am so proud of them!

Today I stand here proudly as a single mom of three beautiful adult children. I have experienced and endured some of the worst hardships, pain and trauma and I am profoundly grateful for them all. I've made so many mistakes, some big and some small. I've been everything that I could think to be for my babies. I've instilled good morals and values in all of them, and I see those fruits coming forth as they grow in their adulthood. I've loved them more than I've loved myself. I've always taught my babies that there will never be any success without struggles, but what they taught me was far more valuable. My faith has kept me from giving up and has pushed me to keep fighting so that my babies can experience the best version of their mama. I believe I've made God happy. He chose me to be their mom because He trusts me, and He knew I could handle it with His help. My faith tells me that for every dark moment, every battle, every hard place and painful storm, my Father in Heaven will never allow us to go through those struggles without allowing them to bring greater hope and purpose. He will always bring us through the fire better, stronger and wiser. Restored, redeemed and renewed. He's always with us. He is the light in the darkness. He never leaves us to fend for ourselves in challenging times. That's His promise. We may feel alone, but we are never alone. He's always there. Allow your faith to believe.

A Love Note to All My Single Mamas:

Self-care is self-love. You must take care of and love yourself first so that you can love your child the way they need to be loved and cared for—and so you can give them the best version of yourself. You are your child's superhero, and often they see perfection when they look at you. No one is perfect. You will make many mistakes and even disappoint them unintentionally, and it's ok. It is important your child understands this. Effective communication and listening are imperative to support a healthy relationship with your child and it will also help them with their social skills and communication with others. Last, when things get to be too much and you feel overwhelmed, STOP, PRAY and BREATHE! These are things that have surely helped me during my journey of motherhood. Love yourself, hold onto this and keep pressing through, Mama! You've got this!

> **Not only so, but we also glory in our sufferings, because we know that suffering produces perseverance; perseverance, character; and character, hope. And hope does not put us to shame, because God's love has been poured out into our hearts through the Holy Spirit, who has been given to us. Romans 5: 3-5, NKJV**

~ Portia Mosby

"Motherhood is the greatest thing and the hardest thing."

– Ricki Lake

Katherine DeLisa Stokes has supported families of children with disabilities since 1999. She became involved in the advocacy world when her daughter was born at 25 weeks gestation and only given 72 hours to live. Lisa's work not only involves the child/adult but extends to the network that supports the child.

Raising two daughters as a single mother has been challenging and rewarding. Lisa was fortunate enough to have a strong the village. However, she realized that not everyone had this experience.

For the past two years Lisa has continued the work of helping others, but she has done so with the theme of "Putting the oxygen mask on first mentality".

The most important way to be an advocate is by speaking up. Lisa is an advocate for everyone. She stands with courage, grace, and conviction.

She's INTENTIONAL.

JUST A CONVERSATION WITH GOD
LISA STOKES

You don't know my story! You have no idea what I've been through! Truly, at the nifty age of 50, I am finally at a clear understanding of what it means to be totally connected to the King. I was a pew baby, growing up in church all of my life, but not fully understanding the power of a connection with the Master. Quote a few scriptures, mumble the Lord's Prayer—yes, I could do that! But as time went by and life caught up with me, I found myself at the lowest of lows and darkest of pits, in search of that very same God I learned about in church. But right now, at the beautiful half-century mark, my relationship with the Lord is in check and I'm heaven bound. This journey didn't come without some bruises on life's roller coaster ride.

At this moment, I am crystal clear on the importance of family and parenthood, particularly with the honor of being the parent of a beautiful human being who was uniquely designed by God. My precious gift, Mariah, burst into this life weighing a whopping one pound at birth. I got to witness the masterful handiwork of God as He developed her tiny little body right before my eyes. It was so personal but excruciating to watch at times! I watched my daughter's little eyelashes come in. I watched parts of her body, still transparent, develop. Her skin was like the delicate pages of the Bible; you had to be extremely careful when you touched it. This sight, this scary but beautiful view, was complex and daunting to experience from the eyes of a young mother. From my helpless vantage point as Mom, I prayed like I never prayed before. At times, my words didn't make sense and were outright disrespectful. The conversational lines of my prayer language went from anger, helplessness, hopelessness, and disdain to one that has now evolved into a solid love relationship with the Lord. I needed to *just have a conversation with God* – a heart to heart, unfiltered talk with Him where I could open up my heart and pour out to Him. This was the toughest prayer moment, but the very one that changed my life forever. God proved to me what He alone was capable of doing for my daughter Mariah, and in me, without my feeble assistance.

Whew, through it all, only God knew that I was afraid of the unknown. I was unsure and unclear about what life was going to be like. The struggle was real, grappling with how I could parent this delicate life who was struggling to survive. Insurmountable odds continued to stack up against us. The cards in the deck, each time, were not in our favor. I was not ready to accept the inevitable. I began to learn, and learn quickly, that one wrong move – one misstep – one moment of inattentiveness could lead to Mariah slipping out of our hands forever. Overwhelming? My God, YES! Doable? It had to be! I had to dig deep and resolve that Philippians 4:13 scripture to remind me that I—no, I mean WE—are victorious. Defeat was not an option! Thankfully, through the trusting relationship I possessed with God, I could make it. It still could be a WIN-WIN day because His competent hands were on the steering wheel of our journey.

While courageously trying to jump over the hurdles and navigate through the tunnels of this life, one has to embrace all of the experiences that come along the way. Accepting that your life is going to be different is extremely personal. It's humbling and life-altering! Any person who can testify to these words will tell you that these challenges will drive you to your knees. For me, it postured me in a prayer position because reality kicked in! My daughter would never crawl, never walk or run, or enjoy all of those amazing milestones that young children experience. In total transparency, I saw DEATH. I mourned daily even with a child still breathing. I grieved the notion that the normalcy of little girl life would not exist for me. The hustle and bustle of dance classes, being a Cheerleading Mom, doing those memorable Mommy-Daughter moments would not exist for Mariah and me. Traditional school life – not happening for us. The weight of these frightening sentiments obscured my vision and set up roadblocks that seemed difficult to navigate around.

However, one day in the midst of my suffering and struggle, the Lord shook me at my very core and said, "Wake up! Normal, like everyone else, won't be normal for you. So, my daughter Lisa, DEFINE your own NORMALCY!" I felt like a new baby was pushing out of my womb. It was called advocacy. This new concept began to take shape as it became clearer to me. The defeated scales were like cataracts lifted from my blinding eyes, giving me a perfect picture of a plan that needed to be constructed. How was I going to make life count for Mariah, so she could live her very best life even in her present condition? My paradigm shifted to focus on her ability versus her inability. Despite her complicated medical diagnoses, Mariah had something beautiful to offer this world and it was my responsibility to share it with the world.

This motherhood ride felt lonely. There were times when I was all alone in a crowded space. I was expending all of my love on my daughter with no one to love me in return. If you've never felt the embrace of unconditional love or never seen it in action, it's when you are able to love someone who has the inability to say "I love you back" or give you a hug back. Your love language and posture are unstoppable, but you can't be the beneficiary of the same in return. To me, even without being able to hear Mariah whisper "I love you" or shower me with kisses, true unconditional love for a child with delicate needs propels you to never cease in your attempts to provide the best life possible. It is downpours of love that are continuously dripping from your heart's faucet – yes, that agape love that God demonstrates to us each day, even when we don't deserve it. Call it grace, if you wish, giving and meeting my needs even when I was not worthy of it or understanding why it was coming my way. God finally brought me to a place of accepting my divine appointment as Mariah's mother and exercising every fiber of my being to ensure that she, along with her sisters, would be okay.

Daily, I shouldered the responsibility of giving care to Mariah alone, with a small intimate village of support. Whereas people would periodically offer their spurts of support, I alone lived the role of being the mother of a complex needs child who would require round-the-clock care, 24 hours a day, 7 days a week. At this point, with two girls, the load was heavily pressing on me to care for two distinctly different children. Literally, I was about to lose my mind. I was in over my head, with all types of thoughts running through my brain, particularly in those moments when Mariah's condition grew worse. Hitting brick walls and managing a myriad of emotions, I too was beginning to sink and drown! I became so overwhelmed that I could barely keep my head above water.

My friend, we take *balance* for granted. Many of us presume we can go about our daily lives, from task to task, and not concern ourselves with what we need for basic survival. It's like driving and driving, and never worrying about fueling up until our car is stuck on EMPTY. Introspectively, I had to insert BALANCE into my life and household, allowing me to divide me and my time up amongst everyone who needed me. There was no personal time. I couldn't pack up Mariah and send her to a loved one's house so I could have Me-Time! Long gone were the days of dating and girls' nights out. Balance did not exist for me, and I didn't know how to make it happen.

You see, Mariah's needs were so massive and required so much of my time that I forgot about or was too busy to wholeheartedly meet the needs of my newest daughter, Maiya. I was handling medical issues, coordinating nursing schedules, attending IEP conferences, and meeting the growing demands that came along with Mariah's issues, and it prevented me from showing up daily for my baby girl, who needed me just as much – if not more. You see, the newest princess didn't ask to be born into this "Lisa World" with a big sister who faces innumerable challenges that require much of Mommy's attention. Another paradigm shift had to occur for me: how to integrate Maiya into this "Mariah World," teaching her how to embrace the challenges of a sister who lives with complex needs. Hence, we had to shape Maiya's thinking and understanding of simple nuances – your big sister won't be able to chase after you, play dolls with you, and interact with you as other people can. Obviously, in the early days, Maiya saw no difference between her and her big sister. As children grow and become observant of their surroundings, so did Maiya. Slowly, the shifts in roles began as Maiya became overly protective of her big sister. She assumed the role of Little Momma, wanting to feed her, doing small tasks for her, and helping take care of her. So, I let her! It was amazing to me that without speaking one word, Maiya recognized that her sister needed more care and attention than she did. Guess what? To this day, Maiya has never complained! What a gift! My youngest daughter wanted to play an integral role in her sister's care, wanting to be a helping hand. Therefore, I began teaching her how to assist Mariah, ensuring she watched my delicate and daily routines. Before I knew it, Maiya picked up on everything.

If nothing else was learned on this journey, it was the need for balance. If I didn't acquire this needed skill, it would have been the death of me! Each one of us must learn how to prioritize our needs, yet infuse moments of balance so we don't tip the scales. Life is too valuable to allow it to escape because we're sucked into a dark vat of despair. Planned balanced moments produce meaningful memories for all.

Throughout this journey, my youngest daughter sacrificed much so we all could meet the needs of her big sister. Planned family events, including birthday parties and vacations, were often canceled because of Mariah's illness. But Maiya never complained. I had to intentionally create balanced moments, which are needed in families like ours, to ensure that everyone's needs can be addressed. It takes skill, but it is not necessary for families to thrive. Hence, I created Mommy & Me weekends, fun-filled overnight experiences at local hotels filtered with magical moments for just my Maiya and me. Pillow fights, fingernail painting, popcorn parties, playing with makeup – yes, all of the things little girls love to do… we did it! These purpose-driven moments were uniquely designed to ensure that Maiya understood that Mommy was there for her too and that my undivided attention was all hers. The ultimate goal was for her to grasp that I was her biggest cheerleader and the loudest voice in the room for her, just like I am for Mariah.

The intentional plans evolve into invisible imprints that leave lasting impressions indefinitely. Fast-forward to Maiya's senior year of high school. She hustled into my bedroom, wanting to show me something, but pleaded with me not to become upset. Unbeknownst to all of us, her senior project was titled "The Forgotten Child: The Sibling of a Special Needs Child." I could see why she stressed that I did not become upset at what she was sharing with the world. She asked if she could tell our tumultuous story. Instantly, I witnessed firsthand the champion rise up in Maiya, ready to open the book of our daily experiences. In the end, her beautifully constructed senior project chronicled her personal journey of being the youngest caretaker of a sister battling complex needs. In transparency, Maiya infused jaw-dropping and heartfelt moments of pain and purpose demonstrated by our family to meet the challenges before us. On Senior Presentation Day, butterflies swarmed in my stomach as I sat nervously in the crowd. With every passing second of the presentation, tears began to fall from my eyes, as those carefully constructed Mommy & Me weekends that etched precious memories on the tablet of her heart forever were shared. The teachers cried. The principal wept and her classmates were moved that Maiya was not ashamed to tell her story and share intimate pictures. She proudly showcased her big sister and proved her own resiliency to all in attendance. Everyone was amazed at her work, shared in detail and passionately. This moment solidified for me what balance was all about. It demonstrated that balance, not just for yourself, but everyone who is involved in your equation, it is required for the flourishing of their mind, body, and soul.

Life has taught this girl a whole lot of important lessons. One invaluable attribute that I have struggled to embrace was self-care. Yes, just like other sisters, I was Wonder Woman – making wonder happen for all people at all times. However, as I was making magic for everyone else, I was killing myself on the inside – naturally, emotionally, spiritually, financially. While sitting still in one of my quiet moments, the notion of loving me came into full bloom. Self-care and loving yourself does not denote that you're being selfish. I embraced that concept the hard way. I experimented with it after attending a support group hosted at my church. After intently listening, I began to put the tools into practice. For you, the key is this: you must fall in love with yourself! You are smart and you deserve the "me, myself, and I time." Subsequently, I kicked off my own movie dates, dinner dates, solo walks, and personal vacations. Sometimes we underestimate private time! Self-care time is not, by any means, being selfish but you're actually ensuring the preservation of your mental, physical, and spiritual well-being. You'd better catch the wave!

Hear me, infused in those self-care moments are intimate moments with the Master that allowed me to hear from Him. In the quietness of His presence, I was able to foresee and embrace life's warning signals before I hit a pothole. For me, it was a gut check. I had to learn the hard way that not listening and paying attention to God's signs would result in me drowning in deep oceans. For way too long, I was inundated with special projects, community service initiatives, church activities, special events, and things that kept filling up every space on my datebook and zapping every ounce of my physical and emotional strength. Signs of distress were coming. Detour signs were posted and flashing lights were beaming, but I missed them all! I missed them all, hence leading to a stroke in November 2019. The Lord had been giving me warning signs that my body was tired, but in my mind, I was that hyped-up bunny who kept trying to hop along busily.

Having a stroke at 50 years old changed my life! It changed my life for the better as I almost lost my life. God gave me a second chance to get it right, and believe me this time, I listened! In the doctor's diagnosis, bleeding had occurred on the right side of my brain and paralysis began to set in on my entire left side. I – LISA – instantly had to make an immediate choice to live or die. Trust me, with your back up against the wall and in a moment of crisis, you don't have long to flesh out choices. Time never ceased and my life was on the line. I chose then to live and even now, I still choose to live! People really don't know my full story!!! It was in that moment that everything I faced over the 50 years of my life had flashed before me. The choice was mine, and mine alone! I threw up my hands and surrendered myself completely into the hands of God for His safekeeping. I stand boldly today to say I'm in His protective custody!

Humbly and gratefully, I thank God for giving me another opportunity to get it right. It is incumbent upon each of us to take introspective views of our lives and make conscientious decisions that will shape our lives. To grow and thrive, you've got to factor God into every equation, but remove yourself from others' problems. For me, I choose LIFE for the rest of my life. I have extracted myself from all future projects and decided to live a better, stress-free life within my realm of control. I'm living to live again with Him, but naturally, I'm here to enjoy quality moments with my children and family. More importantly, I want to maximize my intimate moments with Him. Don't squander the precious gifts of life that God has so graciously shared with you. Learn to love yourself beyond measure, and be comfortable in your own skin. You're needed here for as long as God extends life to you; so, fill the rest of your days with the best of your days.

"A mother's love endures through all."

– Washington Irving

 Larvetricus Harris is known by many as Pastor Vee or Coach Vee, but the greatest accomplishment is being recognized and called mom. She is instrumental in causing everyone around her to grow in all aspects of life.

Larvetricus just released her first published book entitled, "A Child's Cry in the Shadow," which shares the testimony of her overcoming many obstacles from a young age to some of her adult life. To better educate herself, she obtained an Associate's Degree of Arts in Business Administration through Strayer University.

As a mother, Larvetricus has the awesome opportunity to raise four children and be a part of the amazing journey of their lives. As a wife, mother, and friend, through God, she tries to find the balance of being everything that people need her to be. She makes it her business to guide, lead, and coach individuals into any possibility that presents itself.

ENOUGH OF THE CHURCH
LARVETRICUS HARRIS

The church is always the place where people come to be revived and refreshed through the written scriptures of God. We recognize that churches are full of excitement, reverence and spirit but the scattered commotion is illuminated by Hammond B3 organs and children. It is a notion that the Pastor's children are the absolute worst, and they have the tendency to be the hellraisers that continue to stir up the most chaos in the church. The Pastor's Kids (PK) have the task of being at most, if not all, church services because they are towed around by the leading parents. Pastor's children do not have much of a social life outside of the four walls of the church building. Most of their time consists of just being in the church house and only being friends with the other kids in the church.

When mischief and mayhem is heard, they always find the trouble children. And more than likely, the ringleader is that one child who is supposed to be the example to the other little children. Why is this an issue? Because of who their parents are, they should just know better. I can hear it even now: "Child… that's Pastor Such & Such's son or daughter acting like that. Now you know they know better…" What is even more thrilling to me is now that my child has been labeled as an unfit church kid, I am no longer a great mother, because I do not know how to control my children when they are being children.

Not only is the child constantly put under a microscope in the way that they act, but there is another silent mandate that the children of pastors and leaders must be involved in every activity for young people sponsored by the church. When the children should be outside playing, involved in sports or just around their neighborhood friends, they are locked into the commitment of the youth choir, children's church, Vacation Bible Study—the list goes on. Why? The parents leave them without any option. You have seen it: Every department that has a lack by default can be filled by a child of a pastor or leader who has no choice but to do it. I want to share why my children will be raised differently than most of the young people I came up with in church.

Coming up in life I was your typical tomboy. I loved playing basketball. I was that chick who played football, climbed trees, and did everything that people thought only the typical male should do. I never had that dream of being rescued by a knight in shining armor. I never had the thought that I would be married, let alone have my own kids. To be honest, I settled for the thought of being single and dying alone. Don't get me wrong, I loved kids and was very happy with being everyone's Godmother, that supporting person who made parents' jobs less difficult.

I did not have the best upbringing in my life. I came from an abusive environment that produced a lot of pain. When I was around eight years of age, my mother left home due to the foul hands and lips of my father. I never thought my mother was weak for leaving, because I had seven and a half years of a mother who spent every hour making her girls feel safe in a rocky situation. But, with everything going on in my household, something in me was refusing to bring children into this world by the way of my canal. Being raised the way that I was raised, I really did not want to bring children into this world through me.

You see, after my mother left home, never to return, the little girl I once was died. I had to grow up quickly; I had to be a grown woman. The duties that my mother had now belonged to me. I was now responsible for all of the cooking, cleaning, and raising my little sister. Being a child, acting like a young lady was not fun. I often said to myself that if this was what life, marriage, and relationships were all about I would kindly dismiss myself from that type of life.

As I got older, even though I was content with being by myself, I still desired connection from others. I still wanted to be in a community where relationships blossomed. I tried the gang, but that was totally exhausting, as it kept you fearing for your life. I could have just stayed home for that; all my family did was drink, argue, and fight. It wasn't until I found a group of individuals inside a church that I felt I could finally associate with people. Not knowing how to swim, I dove into the deep with ministry. I wanted everything and to do whatever it was that I thought God wanted me to do. When the doors opened, I was there. And, when they were closing, I was cutting the lights off to lock the door on my way out. I loved the thought of being wanted.

I cleaned the church, ushered, prayed, fasted, taught Bible study, and led. You name it; I did it. From traveling with other pastors and evangelists from state to state for the Gospel to making sure their Bible was in place for them to preach the Word of God—I mean I loved it. I lost myself in the church, in the building. It was my safe place!

It wasn't until I developed my personal relationship with God that my mind began to take a detour in allowing me to think and take "me" into consideration. Thoughts of maybe having a family one day no longer seemed farfetched. I could envision myself becoming a great mother. I was married May 27, 2006, and through this marriage I was blessed with two bonus children. This seemed a little insane at first, but I realized that motherhood came naturally. Something in me snapped! Question after question flooded my mind on how to assist in raising his children from his previous marriage. Not only did I have two bonus children, but a year after marriage, I had my first son in 2007, then my second son in 2010.

I did not have any experience in raising children and I had no idea how to raise children in church. But one thing I did know was that I would do it differently from what I had seen! I just have to get through everyone trying to enlighten me in what it means to be a mother in the church. Not only am I a mother in the church, I have a title as a pastor that changes all the rules to the game. The first remarks I heard from a woman in the church were "…make sure you raise them in the way to go…and make sure you keep them in church."

Now here I am with my bonus children twenty-two and nineteen, and my boys are eleven and thirteen. At this point, I am asking myself and trying to find the answer to how raising these boys to love God while guiding them to be who they are as young African American men loving God. I now understand that it is not all about the church building and all the activities therein, but the importance of making sure they build their own personal relationship with God.

I can hear it like yesterday when my oldest son, Keith Jr., looked me in the eyes and stated, "I don't really know if I believe in God." While he was saying those very words, my other son Isaiah looked at me as though that gave him an open door to speak his mind. "Yeah, Mom and I am tired of Children's Church. Do we have to go to church every time you go?" A part of me wanted to scream at them and state all that God has done for them. I mean really, do they not realize if it had not been for God on our side, we would not have the things that we have? Come on children, every time you flip the light switch and a light comes on, that is a sign of the blessings of God. You have a roof over your head, clothes on your back, water to wash your tail, and toothpaste to refresh your mouth each morning. I wanted to testify to my sons like we were in a testimony service proclaiming how good our God was, is, and will be. They must have forgotten who I was and what I stood for; I mean, I am the Pastor Larvetricus Harris! Right when I was getting ready to open my mouth, it was like God Himself snatched the words from my mouth...

Wow, I thought to myself. *Come on, pastor, preacher, evangelist, Coach Vee; how do you respond to this?* At that moment, while taking a deep breath, I laid aside all titles people referred to me by and began to coach myself. I have the tendency at times to be more to my children than they need me to be. My sons need Mom and nothing more! It is easy to teach and guide others from the outside to trust God, but nobody taught me the balance of building relationships from within the four walls of the personal space I reside in. All this time, I have been setting an expectation on myself based on others' relationships with God. Wow, Larvetricus, wake up the mother in you and talk to your sons! Come on girl, enough of the church!

When I state enough of the church, I am not saying do not go to the building to worship, I am simply stating the fact that there is more. More of what? More than just carrying a title before or after your name, more than the prestige that these titles may hold—sweetheart, there is just more to the church than everything that goes on inside those walls. Where is the balance of me being who people need me to be based on what God has called me to do versus just being the mom that my children require of me?

I am so glad that my children only expect me to be Mom—nothing more, nothing less. They do not care about the title before my name nor the weight of the position. So instead of trying to fix and maneuver around the expectations of others, I decided to live by something I have already been delivered from, and that is people.

Why enough? The standard of church has been so demanding that the children have never been able to engage in a social life. I can only imagine that after the return of the grades from a test, the teachers hear "thank you, Jesus!" as a response. When the children are supposed to be enjoying life, they are burdened down with the affairs of the church. In the organization I was a part of, everything was a hell issue. If you wore pants, you were going to hell. If you wore makeup you were going to hell. Do not ask to go to the movies or even skating. I was forbidden to go to the movies or skating—why, you were going to go to hell! Do not even mention going on a vacation, unless it was some type of Christian retreat for young people. I felt like Oprah Winfrey when she gave everybody cars – you are going to hell, you are going to hell, everybody is going to hell!

With what I had coming up in church, I had to find a more excellent way for me and my household. I begin to put pencil to paper and plan out how I was to change my thought process. I refused to raise my children in church the way I came up in those walls. As the plan began to unfold, I had to first learn what my children's interests were. I stopped talking at them and began to talk to them and with them. More importantly, I had to be intentional with my listening as I learned what they actually liked doing. Boy, did that blow my mind! Even to this day, I can have wonderful, heart-provoking conversations with all four of my children. I have truly learned what they like and dislike, what they enjoy and what they do not enjoy. I was so determined to get this right, I aided in coaching my children in sports. Oh…I am one of those parents and leaders who will miss a church meeting to go to a parent-teacher conference at their school.

With everything that I do within the church, I took the focus off the building and the legalism inside, and I simply teach my children the value of having a personal relationship with God for themselves. Does this excuse them from volunteering to be active in the things within the walls? Does this mean that my children can do what they please and not go to church? Of course it does not! But it does not hold them hostage to the silent demands either.

Please do not get it twisted! My children still must show up and participate in some of the church activities. They still have the responsibility to get involved in the community within the walls of the church. One of the things that our church teaches is that "Life Is Better Connected." We are a community that believes in building non-judgmental relationships. We do not just act like a church; we have become the church.

I do have to bring out the fact that there is a rule in my home that my children realize that missing church is not an option. Sounds contradictory, doesn't it? As a parent, I do realize that I must raise my children in the way to go, so when they come of age, they will learn to stand for something. Responsibility must start somewhere, beyond just cleaning their room and keeping their grades up. Each of my children are leaders, and what good are leaders if they first do not know how to follow?

I often wonder if I am being an effective parent and mother with my boys. Am I teaching them the ways in which they should go? Am I being a great example? Will they be great leaders, and will they succeed in life? Should I be harder on them based on their skin color and everything that they are going to have to face in their future?

My two youngest asked me to take them to the mall, because during that week we had not had a chance to spend a lot of time together. Me being me, I agreed. Plus, this would give me a great opportunity to catch up in conversation with them.

I must tell you; this was one of the greatest conversations I have had with my children. I could see that something was bothering them. My youngest took the lead, while my oldest had this look on his face that was quite alarming. As they begin to speak, my youngest explained to me that it was time for an increase in their allowance. What! Why? At that point, my oldest, in his cool voice, stated, "Ma, I feel like what we do at church is our job and we need to be compensated for it."

The nerve of these children, I thought to myself…

Let me explain: My children get an allowance of around $100.00 weekly. Oh, stop it, let me explain! Before you totally think I am crazy or rolling in some type of mad cash, I am not. I take taxes out of my children's allowance: Social Security tax, Medicare, health & dental insurance, and the 10% of tithes. Now that they wanted an increase, I explained to them that I must deduct additional fees, such as 401K, Wi-Fi and cell phone usage. While they had been getting about $40 a month, they are now bringing in around $20 a month. It was after this that I found out that my children do have a personal relationship with God. You should have seen them, or should I say heard them, talking to God about me. My youngest stated in his bedtime prayers, "God, why is my mom acting so outlandish with our allowance?" It was then that I realized that I was headed in the right direction by teaching them to focus on their relationship with God.

I had to take a page out of my own book and coach myself. I had to learn that is it okay not to be at every church function or meeting. A great friend told me recently to learn how to take a rain day and do nothing but enjoy myself with whatever it is that I want to do. I am finally at a point that the scale of my life is balancing itself, as I allow God to order my footsteps and trust Him. Just think—it took over twenty years to learn how to enjoy me. What freedom it is to be delivered from people.

I no longer allow my mind to be cluttered with the egotistical ways of others within church. I am now able to coach my children beyond just parenting them. They understand to the fullest that I am Mom, but beyond that they also know that they have an awesome friend in me. Yes, yes, yes, my children will and do get on my nerves, but I love them to life! It just took me saying enough of the church to realize the importance of ministering to my own children when they need me. What good is it to gain the whole world and lose the very people that you bore? Enough of the church saints!

"Moms are the people who know us the best and love us the most."

– Unknown

 Jackie Taylor Powers is a God-fearing woman, a wife, a mother, a survivor and a first-time author. Together with her husband of 13 years, Jeremiah, they have a beautiful blended family.

Jackie was born and raised on a farm in a small rural town called Hustle, Virginia. She loves spending time with family and friends and supporting their son in his many sporting events. She also loves traveling and creating lasting memories along the way.

Jackie has a passion to help other grieving mothers survive with the loss of a child. She is the Founder and President of Khadijah's Scholarship Foundation, a 501(c) non-profit organization created in loving memory of her daughter Khadijah. Living with great losses, depression, and fear she has decided to turn her pain into purpose and tell her story.

TOMORROW WILL BE BETTER
JACKIE POWERS

Never in a million years would I have imagined living in this world without my baby girl. She was my everything, the reason I hustled so hard. We had big dreams of conquering the world together. I knew when I gave birth to my daughter Khadijah at the young age of 18, life would not be easy as a single mom. My plans to attend a four-year college wouldn't be possible. I was not going to leave her for my mother to raise. I wanted to be there for her every first: her first words, her first steps, her first fall and to wipe every tear away. Although life didn't go as planned, I attended and graduated from the Braxton School of Business in the legal administrative program. I was able to provide for her despite my circumstances.

I never gave up on all my dreams after being a single mom. I still wanted to travel and see the world. I grew up on a farm in a small rural area that didn't have much to offer. I wanted to live in a big city where I could raise Khadijah with more opportunities. After visiting Atlanta, Georgia several times we decided this was the move for us. In July 2001 my best friend and cousin, who also had a daughter, and I moved over eight hours away from home, the only thing we knew. I was always one to take risks. I always had the confidence of knowing I would somehow make it work and most of all, I had a praying grandmother.

I had saved just enough money for the move, not knowing where my next paycheck would come from. See, I did not have a job offer when I left Virginia, but by the time I reached Atlanta I had a call from the temp agency to start at a prestigious law firm first thing Monday morning. Everything seemed to be working out in my favor. I had a great job, we lived in Buckhead, a nice ritzy and safe neighborhood, and Khadijah loved her new school. It was easy for her to make new friends. She was always kind, with a bubbly personality. Now don't get me wrong, she had a diva attitude but was an all-around great kid. She joined the cheer team and completed her first language arts class, French, by the second grade. We found a church; although much bigger in size and numbers than our hometown church, the spirit was just the same. We came back home to visit often. In the beginning it was almost every other weekend, every single holiday and of course she would spend spring and summer breaks with her Grammy. Khadijah was my mom's first grandchild, so they shared a special bond that not even distance could break.

It was the beginning of the summer in 2003 and just like always Khadijah was off to spend her summer with my mom. Shortly after being back in Virginia, she began complaining of a few headaches. Although it didn't seem like anything serious my mom took her for a checkup with her previous pediatrician. Nothing out the ordinary was found, not even in her bloodwork. I thought maybe she was feeling a little down because she missed me, so I surprised her with a quick weekend visit. A week later, on Father's Day, I received a phone call from the emergency room doctor at Riverside Tappahannock Hospital asking for my permission to transfer my daughter to VCU/MCV Trauma Center. With not a lot of explanation at the time, I gave my permission and I immediately booked a flight home.

When I arrived at the hospital that evening, I'll never forget the look in my mother's eyes. The doctors explained to me that we needed to have an MRI of her brain. After waiting all day to take the MRI, what seemed like an eternity, within a blink of an eye my life changed forever. There I was standing at the nurse's station when the doctor said, "Miss Taylor, your daughter has a brain stem glioma and her prognosis is one and a half to two years' life expectancy." The sound of my cry pierced my ears. I dropped to my knees and I remember her Godfather picked me up and we were taken into a consultation room. The doctor showed the pictures from the MRI and began speaking a lot of medical terminology. Nothing he said made any sense to me. Did he just tell me my baby girl had less than two years to live?

The rest of that night was a blur. I got into that small hospital bed with her and I just held her in my arms all night. Immediately my emotions were all over the place. I was angry, I was sad, I couldn't stop crying. I began blaming myself. I asked God…why me? My daughter was the perfect child. She was beautiful. She had an infectious smile. She was an old soul who loved everybody. She used manners to her elders. I could not understand how a healthy and happy child could end up with a tumor the size of a grapefruit on her brain stem with very little warning, and no definite answers. The doctors describe this as a being a very rare type of tumor. I thought I had done everything right. The worst feeling in the world is knowing that your child is in pain and there's nothing you can do to take that pain away. I never told her the prognosis. I never believed in the prognosis. I wanted to believe that the God I loved and served could not take away from me the most important part of my life.

Immediately we moved back to Virginia, not only to begin her medical treatment, but I would need all the help and support from everyone who loved us. For the next year and three months, it was like living in a never-ending nightmare. We began six weeks of radiation, traveling back and forth each day. One of the great things about being from a small town where everyone knows everyone is the love and support you receive from the community when you truly need it. We had transportation provided for us every day for the one-hour one-way drive. Some days were okay, so we made the best of it, stopping to get ice cream or dining at her favorite restaurant, Red Lobster. Some days even the motion of the car ride made her nauseous and she would be so weak. We had so many doctor appointments; we even participated in a trial procedure at NIH in Bethesda, Maryland to possibly slow the growth of the tumor. I was willing to go any and everywhere. We received a second opinion from Dr. Ben Carson, who at that time was the head neurosurgeon at Johns Hopkins. The diagnosis was the same. We reached out to St. Jude's Hospital and was told there was nothing they could do. Because of its location surgery was not an option.

The radiation did what it was supposed to do. The tumor shrank, and for a minute it was almost like being normal again. She had started having more good days then bad. She was happy. We were able to travel to Disney World at the expense of the Make-A-Wish Foundation. Although I had taken her to Disney before, this trip was truly magical for her. She was treated like the royal princess she was. It was an experience for the both of us and we were able to take my sister and niece to make lasting memories that I hold so dear to my heart. Seeing her smile again the way she did before the diagnosis was priceless. For just one week she had no doctors, an adventure every day, and yes, ice cream for breakfast. Shortly after that trip and right after her tenth birthday on January 10 things began to change. The tumor started to grow again, rapidly.

With everything going on, her spirit began to change. She had moments where she was angry. Her physical looks changed but she was still the most beautiful angel here on earth. She was tired more often. She was sad about not being able to run and play like normal. She was now dependent on a wheelchair for mobility. She always loved school, so not going wasn't an option. After a meeting with the school board committee, knowing the great risks involved, she was approved to attend her fifth-grade classes. If it were up to me, I would have kept her with me every second of the day. I never realized how much I needed that time just to release my thoughts and tears. Being strong in front of her had started taking its toll on me. I was watching my baby girl slip away day by day. What do you say when your child says, "Mommy I don't want to die?" Anger began to set in again. My faith began to waver. I was scared. I couldn't protect her from the world. I couldn't stop the looks and stares she received when we were out in public. I couldn't stop the whispers and yes, laughs from the children at school. After only a couple of weeks of school she simply could not go any longer. She never gave up. She was a fighter. Soon thereafter, she was placed on hospice care and I had to execute a do not resuscitate form; that was the only way I could keep her home with me and not be admitted to the hospital.

It began to be all too real, the diagnosis, the prognosis, this reality I was living. My every thought was a silent prayer. I didn't have time to stop and think about myself. My feelings or anybody's feelings other than Khadijah simply did not matter. I had to make sure she knew just how loved she was. I remember asking God, *If you are real and you are a God of miracles why can't you heal my baby? How could You let her suffer? God, where are you and when are you going to show up? I need you.* God knew I was not only struggling with losing my daughter, I was struggling with losing my faith. You see, this was not my first loss. I lost my brother when I was eight years old. He was killed in a bad car accident his senior year, a couple of months before graduation. He was a passenger in a car that was hit by a drunk driver going in the wrong direction. I had also lost my father due to heart failure. Even though my parents divorced when I was two, he was always there. I spent every weekend with him growing up. He was my protector, the one who spoiled me. I could always count on him to be there for me, until he wasn't. I felt like God had turned his back on me. I felt like he didn't care.

I will never forget that Thursday morning, the last day that Khadijah could talk. We had been listening and singing to Whitney Houston's song "I Love the Lord" all morning when she said to me, "Mom, I think it's time for me to write my dying wish." My heart broke into pieces. I was shocked and in disbelief, but she did not have one tear in her eye, not a tremor in her voice. Without letting her know my state of mind, I asked her, "Why honey, do you see angels?" She said, "No, but His hand is on me," and I said "Who, whose hand is on you?" That's when she told me that God had his hand on her. I called my sister to come over, and my mom had just got back to the house. For the rest of the day we just held her.

It was now one week after she could no longer talk or no longer eat and I whispered into her ear, "It's okay, baby; Mommy will be okay." Even though I knew I would not be okay, I couldn't watch her suffer anymore. I had to let her go. She passed away peacefully less than 24 hours later with me and her family right by her side. On October 1, 2004, she gained her heavenly wings and a piece of my heart was forever gone.

There are no words that can explain the loss of a child, whether the loss is due to illness, an accident, or by any other means. The pain is the same. It cuts deep with a never-ending bleed. My soul became numb, my days turned into nights. Thoughts started to take over my mind and I began to wonder, *Lord, what is my purpose? Why am I still here?* I began professional therapy to help me through my darkest days. Not one of them understood what I was going through. Each time I had to relive the pain in telling my story. I could not take another session, so I stopped going. It wasn't until I went to group therapy with other parents who had lost a child just like me that I began to feel some sort of relief, comfort. They felt the same pain that I felt. Just listening to and hearing others gave me hope for tomorrow. It took a long time for me to tell my story. Other mothers would reach out to me just to talk, or they needed a listening ear. The tears never stopped, but here I was strong enough to start talking through my pain. My pain became my purpose.

Even now, after 16 years, I still have bad days. Her birthday and death date, which happen to be the same numbers, 110 and 101, are especially hard. I often think about all the things we never got to experience, like teaching her to drive a car, or how to apply makeup, all her special senior moments, homecoming, prom, and the list goes on. Her senior year was very emotional to say the least. I began thinking about what I could do to have her remembered with her original classmates' graduation ceremony. With little thought and a lot of support, my husband and I hosted our very first Car/Truck & Bike Show. The money we raised was awarded to one of her classmates for a scholarship to go to college in her memory, the first KSF award. We went to the graduation and were able to present the scholarship to the winner. In addition to that, a memorial page in the senior yearbook was dedicated to her by some of her classmates. My mission was accomplished; her name was announced and although I could not see her walk across that stage, this was a new beginning of many years to come. Planning this event gave me so much joy. With the outstanding support from our #teamdijah and the whole community, it became an annual event, with this year being our 10th Annual Car/Truck & Bike Show. Khadijah's Scholarship Foundation is now a 501(c)3 Non-Profit Organization. Because of Khadijah's love for school and the dream she had to go on to college, this foundation keeps her memory and legacy alive. Although it's very personal to me, it has also helped 21 recipients receive over $37,000 to further their education. Every year I'm reminded that it's not just me and her immediate family who miss her but the entire community, with people coming from as far as South Carolina and Georgia to attend.

I'm often reminded how precious life is. Never take anything for granted and love and cherish each minute. I never thought my story could help someone until that someone said, "Thank you. I did not want to live this life anymore but if you can do it so can I." I've been asked so many times…How do you move on and live without your daughter? My answer is her spirit lives on in and through me. She continues to be the reason I live my life and strive for better. She made me the mother and woman I am today. I now have a healthy, happy and handsome 12-year-old son who looks just like his sister and two beautiful stepdaughters. I don't know what tomorrow holds but I do know Who holds tomorrow. Every day may not be a good day but Tomorrow Will Be Better.

Angela Middleton-Cornish is a transformational leader, successful businesswoman and an inspiration to many. She is the Chief Executive Officer of Middleton & Associates, where she has leveraged over 30 years of business knowledge to educate others in the area of personal development, Real Estate Investing strategies and financial literacy. As a result of Angela's innovative leadership, business, and financial coaching: individuals, teams, and organizations are inspired to maximize their fullest potential, reach their financial goals, and execute their dreams.

Angela is dedicated to inspiring others to see their full potential and transform their lives in ways they never imagined. Her ultimate goal is to help them fulfill their purpose on purpose. Angela is an impactful change agent, whose experiences range from facilitating professional learning events and being the keynote speaker for different industries throughout the East-Coast.

Angela is an intellectual and virtuous woman of extraordinary faith, vision, talents, and presence. Her accomplishments have allowed her to obtain a plethora of recognitions and awards.

Angela's journey to greatness exemplifies that success is a "journey and not a destination." Through this journey, Angela's desire is to inspire others with her walk, encourage them with her talk, and to elevate with her giving.

Angela.Cornish@aol.com

PURPOSE OF A DREAM
ANGELA MIDDLETON-CORNISH

My Secret Place

In the corner of my room on my bed was my sanctuary. As a teenager, sitting on my bed journaling was a regular pastime for me. I would dream about the life I wanted. I shared a room with my twin sisters. I dreamed of having my own room and my own house. I dreamed of getting married and having a daughter first and a son second, of being a businesswoman and inspiring people all over the word.

As a teenager, I remember feeling inadequate, with a burning desire for harmonious relationships and a deeper insight into life. I often daydreamed about how to use my creativity. Ideas were always flooding my brain, which brought on many questions. I always prayed to God with 'what, when and how come' questions. I had the understanding that God had a purpose for my life, and my desire was to fulfill it.

Awakening

I remember one specific day I was daydreaming and praying. This day was a pivotal moment. It finally came to me that it was ok that I did not have it all together. It is ok to be unsure about life. I do not have to come up with all the answers. It was a release of control and a relief of a burden that I carried. I relinquished the thought that I had to have a positive outcome in every situation. At this moment being perfect was not realistic. You will mess up sometimes, and it is ok. God has all the answers. All I must do is believe and live by faith. I knew from this day forward I was created for and with a purpose. I wanted to fulfill that purpose. God became tangible to me. God will not leave me, he will complete what he started, he did not bring me this far to leave me. My God, I felt free—free from my thoughts and free to be me!!

Praying to God often gave me comfort and reassurance. I found myself enjoying the peace and comfort that comes from having a relationship with God. I tend to remember the good. I have trained myself not to dwell on the negative. My mom Jean, my grandmother Gladys and my Aunt Lucile were women who poured LOVE, INSPIRATION and ENCOURGMENT into me. I know that I have the tools to be a successful business woman, wife and mom.

I have seen many positive, successful examples of mothers raising their children with the aid of grandparents, aunts, cousins, daycare providers and neighbors. My mother did an amazing job raising children, whether it was biological, adopted or foster children. She made it look effortless. There are 12 of us now, 33 grands and seven great-grandchildren. We don't have titles among us. We are one big, happy family. I was blessed with many siblings, nieces, and nephews. We all felt much loved and that we were the favorite child. Did my parents do their best? I think so. Now it's my time to use what I saw my mother do and put it into practice.

When it came to being a mother, I took my pieces of parenting styles and created my own puzzle. I took some of my parents' teaching. I caught some things through observation. I adopted my family's strong morals and work ethic with my own philosophies and put God first.

My daughter was my first child; she is absolutely beautiful. The first week she did not open her eyes. The second week she opened them at night. She was a great baby; she didn't cry a lot. I dressed her like a princess. Everything had to match. Her hair was always in cute styles. Her laces on her sneakers had to match her barrettes in her hair. My mother-in-law told me I would get tired of dressing her up like a doll baby, changing her clothes multiple times a day. I never got tired and loved to capture her moments on film or video. My daughter's dad and I divorced when she was young.

Mindset

My mindset was 'nothing can stop me.' My daughter will not lack anything. I found myself giving her a lot, overcompensating for her father not being in her daily life. I was determined that she would be a strong, independent self-sufficient, wise, God-fearing little girl, young lady, and woman. My child's wellbeing was my priority. My friend made a statement to me that her mother taught her, "You should raise your children so other people will like them."

It was important to teach her about money: how to count it, save it and use it. I would give her an allowance and she was good at saving it. When I took her shopping, she was able to count her change before the cashier gave it to her.

Let Her Talk

My daughter's personality grew and blossomed. I allowed her strong will to manifest. I remembered a wise woman told me, "I see your daughter's strong will. Your job is to nurture her. Do not break her spirit; when she gets out into the world, the world has a way of breaking you down to a medium." The lady told me how she was outspoken and outgoing but her mother broke her spirit and she speaks softer now, isn't opinionated and became a different person. I allowed my daughter to give her opinions and have a voice. Her creativity was welcomed and accepted.

Frequent Flyers Miles

Most summers she would visit her grandmother and father in Georgia. I felt it was important for her to have a relationship with her father and his family. I would fly her to Georgia in the summer, and he would fly her back. My daughter's grandmother and her father's side of the family adored her. It was easy to allow her to have a healthy relation with them.

My thought was, it took both parents' DNA to make up my child, so if there is no harm or danger to my child, then a healthy relationship with her dad helps her grow up whole. Why not allow it?

Lesson Learned

When my daughter was 10 years old, she knew how to cook, clean the house, and wash clothes. I remember my sister Candi and I at the Laundromat, not knowing how to use the washing machine. The attendant had to show us. I wanted my daughter to know how to do more than I did at the age of 10. My mother washed our clothes and did most of the cooking.

A lady who lived in my community was observing me. She told me one day, "I bet you are teaching your daughter a lot." I told her, "Yes, I am." She said, "How do you know what you're teaching your daughter will work? Let your daughter come out and play more with the other children. She will use what you have taught her. She will let you know what she has learned outside. Then you will know if what you taught her works. If you need to adjust anything, you do the adjusting." Great advice. Children do not know how to hide what they learn. They will use it like they're doing a neat trick.

Finding Her Purpose

My daughter participated in numerous activities; cheerleading, church, and soft ball were a few. She was self-sufficient, outgoing, and outspoken. She was gifted and anointed. She loved children and used her creativity to teach them. I remember we were at church and this specific day, Sunday school was a teacher short. They asked my daughter to teach. She did an amazing job. That was not the last time she was asked. She could teach multiple groups of children at the same time and the parents' approval rate was high. She was a big help with her bother and over-protective of him.

I remember when she decided private school was not for her anymore. She pleaded her case and won. The adolescent years had some bumps, hills, and valleys. My friend Stephanie and I would use each other when we needed our girls to get a message that they were not catching. Your children do not always hear your voice. Find someone they trust. It's like gospel to them when they hear the same message from someone else. They will come back and talk about the idea like it was theirs.

Purpose

It was truly a blessing to watch her grow up and evolve into her own person. She had friends, she enjoyed high school, and her graduation and prom were exciting. Her peers looked up to her and she had a no-nonsense way of life. My daughter realized she was good at teaching and pursued a teaching career. She is pursuing her purpose. She went to her Grandma Jean's alma mater, Coppin State University. She became independent, with many accomplishments.

A mother-daughter relationship is precious.

My Son

I remember the words: "You are pregnant. It is positive." I heard from the second test. My thoughts were pure joy. The same day I found out I was pregnant was my family vacation to the ocean. We had an amazing time. My cousin said, "You sure look great in that two-piece bathing suit. I can picture that lime green and purple dotted bathing suit. Little did I know it would be years before I was in two pieces again.

At the beginning of my pregnancy, I had morning sickness. Thank God my daughter was not squeamish. When she heard me gagging, she would run to my side to assist me with a trash can. What great help she was. As the months went on, the morning sickness subsided. My craving while pregnant with my daughter was peanut butter cup candy; she is not fond of that candy at all. My craving with my son was popsicles. He does like popsicles. I feel it's definitely ok to give into some of the cravings you may experience—something in moderation if you are not harming you or your unborn child.

It was amazing to see my stomach grow to an enormous size. This pregnancy was much different from the first pregnancy. As my body transitioned, there was no doubt I was having a large baby. I was at the end of my pregnancy. My stomach stretched to my knees and my lap had disappeared. My son had no more room in my stomach.

The due date was scheduled, an emergency C-section followed by a new healthy baby boy. What a beautiful sight. I had two children now; how would I share the time, love, and energy? I loved my first born so much. My heart opened and another chamber was instantly created. You love the second as equally as you love the first child.

You Got This

A mother's instinct is like jump-starting a car. You are pushed in gear. You are on auto-pilot and you start figuring things out. The agape love is present and all the worries of having two children go out the door.

Having a strong support system for new moms is imperative, whether it's their first or their fifth child. The family should observe their health progress, whether it is mental or physical health. Both need to be monitored. My Grandmother Ladybird stayed with me for two weeks, while my daughter stayed with her babysitter. It gave me so much recovery time, some me time and some bonding time with the newborn. I needed it all. My body had gone through an ordeal.

Schooling

I stayed home three years before I went back to work. Clifton was a fast-growing baby. I was looking for a traditional christening outfit. For my son's size I found a three-piece suit, size 2T, at the age of six months. Clifton grew mentally and physically at a rapid rate. He learned quickly. He was fond of football.

I asked my father for advice. What is the one thing I should be teaching my son? He told me to teach my son to sit. He said, "We are naturally athletic, with a lot of energy. When your son goes to school and he's not used to the school structure of learning, he will be labeled. Children are forced to sit most of the day. It goes against how we learn, how we are designed and wired." My father said, "If he can sit at home then he can sit in school."

When Clifton was one year old, I implemented my father's advice. I changed my son's bedroom and designed it into a classroom. He had a table and chair for his desk. The alphabet letters were in cursive and print across the top of his wall. All kinds of posters that would be in a first-grade classroom were in his room. I taught him with the Abeka program, and he and his sister learned to do sign language. He learned his alphabet, how to write and sound the letters out and write in cursive before kindergarten. He skipped the first grade and did well in the second grade. They soon gave him third grade work to keep him engaged, and he excelled.

Busy Work

Clifton's activity early on was tap dancing. That did not last long, with a family full of football and basketball players. Baseball, basketball, drum, flute, and the saxophone were other activities to keep him busy. Later, he tried football and lacrosse.

We Choose Basketball

Clifton played sports all year long. My husband and I decided that basketball would be the sport to concentrate on. As Clifton grew taller his shoe sizes matched his age. At the age of 10 his shoe size was 10. His feet stopped growing at the age of 17 and yes, his shoe size is 17. He enjoyed all the new sneakers.

As my son grew taller, I found myself educating people on what to say and what not to say. I was amazed at the most inappropriate statements people would make. One tournament we were at, I saw a lady I knew. We talked until the game started. Our children were playing on opposite teams. When the game was over, she had people challenging my son's age, as if I lied about his age and put him on a team with younger children. Our children were the same age. After that, my son had an official state ID card to prove his age.

The Life of an Athlete

Basketball became an added culture in our life. Parents of an athletic child have a busy life. There were many teams he joined at different times. I was a taxicab mom, lots of practices, out of town games, and tournaments. He won many metals, trophies. Our vacations were scheduled around his basketball commitments.

Clifton had to get an ID card from a specific sports organization to play in their summer tournaments. The lady that was checking birth certificates and the IDs from the children looked to be a senior. She looked at my son's ID and said, "Ooooohhh, you have a driver's license. We need to go on a date. Come on, come on when you going to take me out? You can drive." My son put his head down as the other children laughed. I asked her if she had grandchildren. "Yes, I do." "Can you imagine someone sexually harassing your grands?" She said, "Absolutely not." "Well ma'am, what in the world do you think you just did to my son. He is a child and you asked him for a date and made fun of his ID while the other children laughed. I hope and pray you do not encounter someone embarrassing and making a joke out of your grands, like you just did my son." She looked at my son with his head down. Her eyes filled with regret and she was very apologetic.

I had decided early on I would not allow people to put labels on my children. I would educate, and not hate.

High School

At the end of Cliff's 10th grade year, the private school that he attended announced they would be closing. There were many emotions. No 10th grader wants to go to a different high school. The day the school closed, my husband and I had many schools calling us. They heard of the school closure and asked if we would consider their school for Cliff to relocate to. I called a friend and asked her, "Why are we getting all these calls?" She laughed, "You and your husband are the only two people that do not realize your son is a superstar in basketball." "Ok what does that mean?" I asked. "It means that you do not have to worry what high school or college he will be going to." That excited us and we decided on a new high school.

Stories

There are many stories I can write about concerning people's reaction when they saw my son. The reason this is important is because people make statements to children without thinking. That culture of 'I can say what I want to you because you are a child' must stop. Some adults don't take children's feelings into consideration, and they damage children's self-esteem. It got to the point my son would say, "Mom, do not worry about it. You do not have to say anything," or he would say, "Uh-oh, they don't know my mom's getting ready to say something," implying he knew I was ready to educate. Things people would say:

- He is too tall for his age. My reply: "He is not. In my family we are tall, so he is the right size for his age in our family. Now because of his size he would not be in your family, because you are short."

- My, he is a big boy. Now why is it that 300lb people call tall big? I am not sure. I would widen my eyes, looking shocked at their statement. My son and I would look at each other, talk with our eyes, look at them and grin. Sometimes it was not important to educate.

- What do you use for his feet, shoe boxes? Do you have to cut out the roof of your car? My son looked at me, pulled my shirt and said, "Mom, let's go." "No son, I have to say something." My reply: "Ma'am, do you know how hard it is for parents to teach young boys to respect old women like you? You do not know my son." My son started walking to the car. "The words that came out of your mouth did not edify my son. You tore him down with your words. What in the world did you expect the outcome to be from speaking like that to my child? I teach him to respect women like you. Now I must go to the car and heal and build up the place that you just tore down." She cried as I spoke. "Ma'am please, please forgive me." "Ma'am, you did not say it to me. You said it to my son. You should be apologizing to him."

My son learned to enjoy the notoriety he received from being six feet nine inches tall.

From the 5th grade to 11th grade, he was in private school. His last year he wanted to try public school again. He pleaded and won. His 12th grade year he had over 40 colleges sending him letters to come to their school. Praise God!! All our work paid off. He chose a college out of state. Cliff eventually came back to his home state and graduated at an in-state college.

Cliff got his CDL license and was given a dump truck by his dad. He joined the family business. He quickly realized one of his purposes was to teach. He opened up a school to teach people about the trucking business.

No Regrets, Lesson Learned

When I look back, were there some things I wanted to change in raising my children? Absolutely. When I look forward, I thank God for the opportunity to raise healthy children with love. We did not always see eye to eye. But we loved each other.

Have Faith

God's will is perfect. He will give you a glimpse of things that will happen. He will finish what he starts. The enemy tries to stop God's plan. But God is almighty.

I was not always a perfect parent. I learned lessons along the way. I always had a pure, loving motive and a perfect heart. My intention was always through agape love. I learned a lot raising my first child. The second child, of course, had a different personality and there were more experiences. There are different seasons in life when you are raising your children to be adults. The relationship changes, and you are not raising them anymore. You are assisting, encouraging, guiding, and watching. You are seeing what you put in them, what they learned from others. You're witnessing them create their own values. They decide what they want to be and do. They become independent adults.

Prayer Changes Things

I can remember my grandmother Gladys saying, "They're just on your hands; wait until they are on your heart and you are on your knees." I know so well what that statement means. I do more of the latter part now that my daughter and son are adults.

My children were birthed with PURPOSE for God's perfect plan!!

> "If you're a mom, you're a superhero. Period."
>
> – Rosie Pope

 LaTia Reynolds is a divorced, single mother of four. She is the owner and visionary of Single Mommy"ing" It, a brand in which she shares her challenges of her journey in motherhood, and how the Lord has always seen her through.

LaTia believes that by faith, believers can overcome any circumstance that they are faced with. Her mission is to encourage, inspire, and uplift single mothers all over the world by sharing her experiences.

LaTia has found purpose in the ministry that the Lord has assigned to her as she strives to live by the scripture, "I can do all things through Christ which strengtheneth me." - Philippians 4:13, KJV

SINGLE MOMMY"ING" IT
LATIA REYNOLDS

As little girls, we all grew up planning and imagining the life we desired and the wedding of our dreams. We imagined marrying the love of our lives and living in our dream house, all while raising our amazing children. Together! For some, this dream became a reality. For others, such as me, this dream was interrupted when life, with its ever-so-unpredictable self, happened.

My Journey

No one ever dreams of the day they will become a single mother – at least I didn't. Saturday, March 26, 2016 will forever be a day I will remember. It was the day I officially became a single mother.

Now, I'm one who loves getting an understanding of the meaning of words. I do this because so much can be misconstrued and misinterpreted. Merriam-Webster defines the word single as 'only one; not one of several; an individual person or thing rather than part of a pair or a group.' With that definition, my personal definition of single mother is basically self-explanatory – a mother who is raising her child or children alone, rather than part of a pair (both mother and father).

I was married for almost eight years and just like most marriages, things weren't always peachy-keen. We had some happy moments and some not so happy moments. We had our smooth sailing and we hit some rough patches. In spite of it all we did what we were taught; we fought. We did the whole counseling thing, we talked it out, we even learned to communicate better than we previously communicated. But with all the fighting we did to try to save the marriage, things didn't work out and eventually that's when the father of my children walked out on us. So, there I was, left with four children, having to figure out how I was going to continue with life, raising my children, and maintaining a household totally and completely by myself. This life included providing for my children, working full time and continuing with the completion of my Bachelor's degree in Early Childhood Education. Needless to say, I had my hands full, but with the help of God, I was able to manage it all.

The Monday after an eventful weekend started with me having exactly one week to figure out how I was going to get my oldest two children to school while I worked on the other side of town. Because of their ages, I couldn't leave them in the house alone; they were unable to get up in the morning and get themselves ready for school. My youngest two, the twins, went to work with me. I was blessed enough to have that previously arranged since I was employed at a child care center. Thank God! I worried and stressed myself sick about how I was going to get all of this done. At the end of the day, I just wanted this process, this season that I was in, to be smooth, mostly for my children. Some things children shouldn't have to endure or worry about because these things are for adults to worry about. Now that doesn't mean our children won't worry. Children are very smart and they are aware of what's happening around them; they're aware of the changes, they're aware of what seems to be out of their norm. At the end of the day, I just didn't want them to worry about anything because they already had to process what occurred and how our family went from a family of six to a family of five. I wasn't too worried about myself because I knew what God told me months prior. Ensuring that my children were well taken care of was my number one focus. That doesn't mean I didn't cry because there were plenty of nights when my children were settled in their beds for the night, where I had the opportunity to pray and cry myself to sleep. I honestly didn't think—no, I actually didn't believe—I would make it through this season without losing my mind. After all the crying I did, to this day, I don't even know how I managed to have any tears left!

It's amazing how God works things out for us. We worry, we pray, we cry, we fuss, and we worry some more. I'm grateful that through it all, He allowed me to have some amazing people in my life who helped to see me through and to ensure that my children and I were able to adjust to our new normal in a different state, hours away from my parents and siblings. I'm especially grateful for my wonderful parents, who sacrificed and helped me, whether it was financially, when they visited, or when they would come pick my children up.

My Household

After the first week of what I like to call our new normal was over, my children were settled in their new routine. My schedule allowed for me to make it home in just enough time for my oldest two to get off the bus. When we returned home from work and school, we would do homework, talk about our day, have a snack, and play outside. I would cook dinner, get their clothes prepared for the next day, do some housework, and we would get settled in for the night. If someone were to look at us, they would think we adjusted well to the changes – little do they know, those emotions showed up in so many ways that would prove otherwise.

Can we talk about how much of a mess my house was? And I'm not talking about having junk everywhere, I'm talking about the emotions. There was a time during this period where my children didn't know how to adjust to our new normal; they didn't even know how to express what was going on inside them. I believe their way of expressing themselves was verbally, so in a way they were expressing themselves. They were fussing at each other, and not the normal sibling rivalry either. They were at each other's throats about the smallest stuff. Talk about Mommy losing her mind! I didn't know how to handle all of this! I literally looked up to God one day and told Him I could no longer handle this; He had to take control. I knew my children were trying to process it all but I knew that within my heart, the situation was rough and I'm sure very confusing to them, I knew they didn't really understand what was going on. I also told my children they could talk to me about anything. They finally asked questions, which meant we definitely needed to have a conversation where I would have to explain everything to them in a way they could understand. As emotional as I was, I was able to hold it all together while explaining to them what happened on a level they were each able to understand. At the end of the day, I didn't want my children confused. They were children and if I was able to ease their minds, with the help of the Lord, I was going to do just that.

Self-Care

As single mothers, we too often ignore the importance of self-care. In fact, we lack it many times—too many, to say the least. I always believed that if the bills were paid, and your family was fed and well taken care of, this was how things were supposed to be. At least that's what I saw growing up – it's what I watched my mother and grandmother do. They made sure everyone was taken care of, and in the meantime, they neglected their wants, needs, desires, and at times their very own health.

It wasn't until I became so overwhelmed with life that I realized the importance of self-care. I can remember being in counseling. My counselor thought that I was okay; they thought I was processing everything well. The truth of the matter was that it was all a front because I knew if I really told him how I felt, I would've broken all the way down. I wasn't worried about my marriage failing, I was worried about my children. How were they really doing? How were they coping? How were they handling everything that had transpired months prior?

Self-care is taking the initiative to preserve or improve one's health. When it came to self-care, it was a challenge for me. I had a hard time taking time out for myself. This went on for a while, until I became so overwhelmed that I shut myself down. When my phone would ring, most times I wouldn't answer it. When I received text messages, my response would always be short. My mother called me and when I finally answered the phone, she laid me out. Somehow, she always knew what I was going through, and when things became overwhelming for me. A mother's intuition is always right. Being the wonderful mother that she is, she eventually came to pick my children up so they could spend the weekend with her. My house was so quiet, I thought I was going to catch up on some much-needed sleep. Well, that didn't happen! So instead, I decided to use this time to relax, pray, cry, and do some more praying.

As single mothers, it is important that we take care of ourselves. It's okay if you're exhausted and overwhelmed; that's to be expected when you're caring for your little ones and maintaining your lifestyle. How can you be a help to your children if you don't first take care of yourself? Take time out for yourself. Go get your nails done, book that massage, take yourself out for dinner, put the children to bed early, catch up on your shows, or get your hair done. Whatever it is, just make sure you take care of yourself in some way.

My Strength

The day I became a single mother was the day I realized just how much strength I had. I can remember in February 2016—I can't remember the exact day—I was sitting in a counseling session and God in His ever-so-still, quiet voice, whispered to me, "I got you." Ever since then He's done just that.

There were times where I didn't know how I was going to pay my bills. I can remember my children and me coming home one evening when I saw a note on my door from the electric company. My electricity had been shut off due to lack of payment. Talk about being embarrassed. I don't think my children even realized what was happening at the moment; they were just ecstatic with the fact that we were spending the night at my Godparents' house. Talk about an amazing distraction from our current reality!

There was a particular month when I had to make a decision between paying my rent or paying child care. Well, I thought everyone has a heart and understood that we all go through things in life, some hard times, some very rough patches. I made a phone call to my landlord and after that call I thought my landlord would understand this hard time, and since I was never late on my rent before, she would be a little lenient. Let's just say I decided to pay child care and my landlord wasn't happy at all. She actually was about to file and start the eviction process. You know that feeling you get in the pit of your stomach, that nervous feeling? Imagine that exact feeling times ten. I thought I was going to have to pack my bags and move back to Maryland, something I didn't want to do because my children were doing excellent in school, especially my oldest. Prior to us relocating to Pennsylvania, we took him out of public school and enrolled him in a private school because his behavior wasn't up to par. After trying to figure things out and asking my family for help, God laid it upon someone's heart to pay my rent for me. And as always, God reminded me of those three words that would help me in this journey we call life: "I got you."

I had many nights where I cried myself to sleep. Many nights where I prayed asking God to make the load lighter. Many nights where I just wanted to see my way clear. Being a single mother allowed me to see the strength I had within. It allowed me to see just how much of a super woman I actually was. So many people would say to me, "Tia, I don't know how you do it." My response was always, "It's all God" because honestly, it had to be Him.

My counselor gave me this book written by Priscilla Shirer titled *Fervent*. When I tell you, this book awakened my prayer life, it literally saved my life and taught me how to pray fervently.

When I think about all that I've been through, I had to thank God for giving me the strength to endure, the strength to persevere, and the strength to overcome every obstacle that came my way. The scripture that always comes to mind when I go through troubles is Psalm 61:2, "From the end of the earth will I cry unto thee, when my heart is overwhelmed: lead me to the rock that is higher than I" (KJV). That scripture has strengthened me in so many ways. It encourages me in knowing that when things tend to be overwhelming (and in this life, they sometimes are), I can cry out to God. Cry out to the One who will make the load lighter, the One who will see me through whatever situation I am facing. The One who will be there every step of the way.

If It Had Not Been...

Have you ever heard the saying, 'If it had not been for the Lord who was on my side, where would I be?' Well, had it not been for Him, I can literally say I don't know where I would be. God has amazed me in so many ways. There were times where I should've given up. There were times when I wanted to throw in the towel. But God kept me. He's been right by my side through every step of the way.

I mentioned before that I was in school obtaining my Bachelor's Degree. There was a class I failed. For some reason, I couldn't get it together. It wasn't that the class was hard, it was simply because I couldn't focus. I was doing my final and completely gave up. I wasn't performing my best at all and I knew for a fact that I could perform better than what I was. Needless to say, when I retook the course, I was able to pass the class with an A. Now I know you're thinking well of course you passed it with an A this time; you were doing the same work over again. Well, it wasn't that easy because my college didn't allow us to reuse our previous work. Because of this, I basically had to pray and stay focused so I was able to pass.

Encouragement

Things aren't how they were five years ago. Although I still have some areas in my life that require growth, God has always seen and continues to see me through every obstacle that comes my way.

Single mom, I want to encourage you. I know things may be rough right now. The bills may be piling up, the children may be acting out, you may need gas in the car, you may need extra money for public transportation, the children are growing and they need more clothes and shoes. In spite of all that is going on, God's got you.

Life situations may come at us from what seems to be every angle, but hang in there, sis. Things will get better. Take some time out for yourself. Take some time out to pray, cry, and scream. Do whatever you have to do but don't forget to breathe. It's not going to always be easy but I want to let you know that you will make it. God has brought me through in so many ways, so I know for a fact He will do the same for you.

I'm reminded of a story. The Bible talks about Job and how he lost everything. He lost his possessions, his children died, his friends turned their backs on him, Job's wife even told him to curse God and die. Through it all Job knew where his help came from. When his back got up against the wall Job said, "Though he slay me, yet will I trust him." Job declared that although he lost everything. Although his body was vexed with sores. Although he had no friends to vent to. Although he probably couldn't see his way clear, Job knew where his help was coming from. He knew he couldn't give up. He knew God was going to make a way out of no way for him. And God did just that. After Job's season of go through, God restored him double.

This is an example of how God will bring you through—how God has brought me through. We go through so much in life and it seems there's no end to it. Let me encourage you. God's got you and He will see you through. It may look like there's no end but there is light on the other side. Hang in there; you've got this, single mom. You're going to look back and see how far you've come and realize that it was all worth it.

"A mother's love is the fuel
that enables a normal human being
to do the impossible"

– Marion C. Garretty

Tamika M. Decatur is a fervent wife, mother and visionary leader, dedicated to helping others reach their full potential. Although an entrepreneur at heart, her natural gifts of gap analysis and future state planning have led her through a diverse career path of business analysis and implementation management within the Healthcare Benefits segment. Her natural gift of leadership and her desire to serve often manifest through roles of mentorship and community service.

Tamika is a rebel of sorts but is driven mostly by her faith and obedience to God. She prides herself in her ability to think outside of the box and is adamant about breaking generational cycles and leaving a legacy that outlives her time here on earth. She also has a passion for diversity and inclusion and is a bona fide agent of change. Tamika works tirelessly to live out her full purpose and potential and challenges others to do so as well!

YOU'RE NOT MY MOM
TAMIKA DECATUR

There are several things that have the ability to crush you if you aren't aware of the astonishing mystery in God's ability to transform broken things into beauty. For me, it was four words out of the mouth of a ten-year-old boy. These four words struck me like an electrical volt, right after a day of family fun, laughter and what I'd considered pure bliss. "You're not my mom," little Antiwan sarcastically uttered, while turning his back to me and walking away. While I never expected him to call me mom, I also never expected those words to cut me so deeply! Although I laugh when thinking about it now, in that moment, I felt hurt, inadequate, unprepared and worthless. Now these feelings weren't from his words alone, but rather from the shocking reality that my loving deeds, kind intentions and overcompensation weren't enough to produce a warm, tender response from my stepson. I struggled with how I would come to terms with loving this child like my own. Kaleb and I had been doing just fine up until this blended union and I wondered if I'd made a huge mistake in taking on this role.

Prior to meeting my husband, I'd been a single mom of one for three years. I'd worked tenaciously to develop fruitful parenting skills and had a pretty good understanding of what worked with my son Kaleb and what didn't. You might say that I'd found my parenting style, as silly as I now realize that sounds. What I didn't yet know was that this parenting style was not a cookie-cutter recipe for my future stepchildren. I quickly learned that I would need to work tenaciously to now develop additional parenting styles, and that was a challenge to say the least! Was I really about to start this journey all over again, with new children? Would I find purpose in this journey? I ended up landing on the idea that God was using me to be a blessing in the lives of my stepchildren and to be an example for other stepmoms in blended families. However, what I had yet to fully understand was that God would use little Antiwan, along with Keosha, Shekinah and Kaleb, as lessons to continue teaching ME the true meaning of unconditional love through parenting.

The union of my husband Antiwan and me created a blended family of eight. With me came Kaleb, who was four years old at the time. With Antiwan came Shekinah, age seven, little Antiwan, age ten, and Keosha, age nineteen. Little Antiwan came to live with my husband, Kaleb and me. Shekinah lived with her mom and siblings in the state of Washington. Keosha was an adult with two children of her own at the time and lived not far from us in another part of Maryland. In addition to becoming a stepmom, I also became a Mi-Mi (a word for a grandmother who is too fly to be called grandma)! Our blended family dynamic was quite complex. I honestly had no idea what I was getting myself into and I didn't have much knowledge about what it took to fulfill my new roles. I really didn't have any healthy examples of parenting in general, and this kind of stuff is not exactly taught in premarital counseling, although it should be! However, after I pushed through my defeated mindset, I discovered that what I did have was a desire to learn, crazy faith and a commitment to break generational curses and cycles within my family lineage. Fortunately, my husband had the same sentiments. Those four driving forces gave me the determination that I needed to pursue my calling, even through the feelings of inadequacy, defeat, and the various challenges that we would face. Now listen, if I had known that those challenges would include lots of conflicts with my stepchildren's mothers, dramatic acts of rebellion from the children and heavy tension within my own marriage, I'm not sure that I would have jumped that broom! My testimony today is strong though; if God called you to it, He will bring you through it!

My marriage alone has been tried and tested in various ways over the years. You name it; we've probably been through it! That, coupled with the challenges of parenting, have really tested my faith, purpose and calling. I remember times when I would lock myself in the bathroom and just cry. There were times that I'd take a pillow into my closet for the sole purpose of screaming into it. However, with every tear and each test, God was purifying me and building the resilience necessary to fulfill my purpose. It definitely didn't feel good during those times, but in hindsight, it reminds me of the creation of diamonds through intense pressure and heat. Some of the pain was planned, while some of it was self-inflicted through bad decisions or actions, but I can say without a shadow of a doubt that God truly causes all things to work together for the good of those who believe and are called according to his purpose. I'm confident that He can do the same for you!

Over the years, I've learned that the key to effective parenting is the demonstration of unconditional love. It's not about what your children call you or give you in return, but rather about what you give and how you can be an additional blessing to their lives. Unconditional love is a love that is not rewarded based upon what is received. It is freely given, without expectations, and manifests itself through demonstrations of patience, kindness, humbleness, truth, protection and perseverance. It requires grace, grace and more grace and a constant dethroning of oneself. It also requires us to embrace and produce unconditional love through what I call the "S.T.E.P.s of Mom-ing," which are characteristics of Servant leadership, Transparency, Effectiveness and Perseverance. This understanding was a pivotal point for me and now drives my approach not only in parenting but in other relationships as well. While none of us are perfect and we will continue to make mistakes along our journey, it is important that we have pivotal points of reference to hold on to and drive us forward. The "S.T.E.P.s of Mom-ing" are just that and can be added as a supplement to your toolbox and parenting journey!

S is for Servant leadership. This requires us to lovingly lead by example and to serve selflessly while esteeming our children's needs above our own. To do this, we must first develop a solid understanding of healthy boundaries to ensure that our efforts don't breed enablement and cripple our children's growth. We also need to lean on God and a community of like-minded parents to provide support and accountability. You may have to step out of your comfort zone to attain this. The demonstration of servant leadership requires us to listen and empathize with our children and as a stepparent; we also have to challenge ourselves to demonstrate servant leadership in our relationships with our stepchildren's parents as well! It's important to note that this demonstration cannot truly manifest within the internal presence of selfishness.

T is for Transparency. This requires us to humble ourselves and be sure that our children know that while we are trying our best, we don't always get it right. We should be quick to apologize, embrace vulnerability and share some of our own shortcomings while expressing that we'll need their patience and forgiveness often. If your child has never heard you genuinely ask for their forgiveness, how can you expect them to learn how to do so with you or with others? Transparency also opens the window of healthy communication. It produces an environment where our children can feel comfortable coming to us. This is so important, especially in today's times of high suicide rates and unhealthy social media dependencies. Therefore, it is imperative for us to produce this environment; our children's lives may depend on it!

E is for Effectiveness. This requires us to invest in learning regularly and to only adapt to parenting mechanisms that bear tangible fruit. The demonstration of effective parenting means to reject the "because I said so" philosophy and actually measure the outcomes of our parenting. This also requires us to celebrate our children for who they are and to cultivate their strengths while also helping them strengthen their weaknesses. Here's a challenge... When is the last time you read a book on parenting or attended a family enrichment conference? It's true that you will only get out of it what you put into it. Invest into your children by first investing into yourself!

P is for Perseverance. There's no fun way to get through the disagreements, acts of rebellion, tears and sleepless nights, but I can assure you that they are worth it! Perseverance requires you to fix your eyes and intentions on purpose instead of process and to view situations from above ground level. It's no surprise that we will grow weary on this parenting journey. However, what's most important is that we don't give up! What's in your toolbox to help you when times get hard? Is your faith a motivating factor? Have you immersed yourself in a community of like-minded moms or parents? Do you have an outlet? These are all questions we need to answer that contribute to our ability to persevere. Self-care is also imperative to successful parenting! When I'm feeling defeated and struggling to find the strength to keep going, it's usually a telltale reminder that I haven't taken the necessary time for myself.

These STEPs have helped me tremendously in developing solid, fruitful relationships with all of my children. My children love each other genuinely and are a product of the environment that my husband and I forged. Kaleb and little Antiwan have a very special relationship and have grown so much as individuals through their relationship with each other. And guess what? I haven't heard those words "you're not my mom" in years! In fact, I can't get a day's worth of rest without hearing Antiwan call me Mom a million times! Shekinah still lives states away, but I've also developed a healthy relationship with her and we talk every time she visits or checks in. Keosha, and the grandkids visit often and call me just about every other day. I often admire Keosha in complete awe as she continues to transform from that stubborn nineteen-year-old novice that I met years ago into the wonderful woman she is constantly pushing to be and become. When she calls for advice or to vent, I'm always honored to pour into her and watch her overcome whatever is standing in her way.

This last requirement to fruitful step-parenting is usually the toughest for most stepmoms. I've touched on it lightly in the previous paragraphs, but now I'll address it head-on. Remember that unconditional demonstration of love that I mentioned above? You know, that love that is not rewarded based upon what is received but rather is freely given, without expectations and manifests itself through the demonstrations of patience, kindness, humbleness, truth, protection and perseverance? Yes! The love that requires grace, grace and more grace and a constant dethroning of one's self? Well, that unconditional love should be demonstrated in your relationship, or lack thereof, with your stepchildren's biological parents as well. While I realize that every family dynamic is different, we all still have the responsibility of manifesting a spirit of unconditional love toward our stepchildren's biological parents. The key to this is focusing inward on us and not outward on them. We have to take the time to assess and measure our own thoughts, actions and attitudes and really do the work to renew our minds and end goals. We have to understand that our stepchildren are watching us and learning from our every move. In some cases, the demonstration of this unconditional love has to start with forgiveness or an apology but remember what I shared above: If God called you to it, He will bring you through it! Here lies an opportunity to really experience the astonishing mystery in God's ability to transform broken things into beauty!

If you'd asked me how I imagined my relationships with my stepchildren would have turned out back then, I would have probably laughed in your face! But to my surprise and through God's grace, we have truly developed something beautiful that I'll cherish until the day I die. I've also learned to love my stepchildren's biological parents as well, and I pray for them often. I am forever grateful to them for blessing me through their children. Listen, navigating the complexities of raising a family is a challenge in and of its own. When you factor in the elements of blending your children and family, it seems almost impossible. However, I am here to tell you that it is not impossible! It requires faith, diligence, hard work and desire. It requires a solid understanding and demonstration of unconditional love. It requires STEPs of Servant Leadership, Transparency, Effectiveness and Perseverance. It requires a lot, but it's definitely possible! In fact, ALL THINGS are possible for those who believe.

Shekinah, Antiwan and Keosha, I love you immeasurably and I thank you for embracing me and for teaching me what the true meaning of unconditional love really is! To my husband Antiwan, I am so blessed to have you as a partner in this thing called life and I love you and our children more than words can say! And to all of my fellow fearless, dedicated stepmoms out there, keep pushing, loving, growing and demonstrating God's love in your family! Keep your toolbox handy and be sure to grow your community! Last, I'd like to leave you with this prayer that I hope you will make your own and use as a tool on your journey to fulfill your purpose of effective step parenting…

God, thank you for calling me and equipping me to be a stepmom. Thank you for the children that you have gifted me and called me to raise. I pray that your love would manifest through me daily and that I would be a demonstration and an example of effective parenting every day. I pray that you would teach me and shape me and provide the strength that I need. Please cover my children daily. Protect them and keep them from harm's way. Let your will be done in their lives, that they may grow to become effective parents of their own and be the change the world needs to see. Thank you for my stepchildren's biological parents. Please bless our relationships and engagements with one another and demonstrate your ability to transform broken things into beauty through us! Please bless my family and every family that we will encounter along our journey. Live big in us and let us be an example to all. Amen!

 Danielle M. Batiste is a mother, bestselling author, speaker and advocate. Danielle is a native of Louisiana, but currently lives in Newport New, VA with her son.

Danielle is a Veteran and knows the pitfalls that the life of a solider can bring to the family unit - especially the effects of a parent being deployed, in the mind and emotions of a child. In her book, "Cryin' Out -Separation Anxiety and The Solder's Child " - she shares the wisdom of her own family's experience.

Danielle is a woman of purpose and cause; thus, her sophomore solo literary project is also one of educating and advocacy. Her book "Let Go My Glucose - Winning with Type 2, was the master mind for her to start her business, Diabetes Made Better, LLC. Her goal and mission as a type 2 diabetic is to Educate and Empower diabetics to live, feel, and look good without living for the numbers. Her accomplishment has been traveling overseas to Germany and Paris for book signings and speaking engagements.

Favorite quote: Be yourself, everyone else is already taken.

PARENTING WITH BIPOLAR DISORDER

DANIELLE M. BATISTE

Being a mom and living every day of your life with bipolar disorder and anxiety is excruciating, to say the least. You want me to be transparent? That is my middle name. Well, let me tell you, this is an uphill battle for me, one that I battle alone due to my stubbornness. I was diagnosed before my baby came along but no one could get me on the right blend of medications so my moods were all over the place. I became manic and sometimes I would stay in that mood for two weeks at a time. So how could I deal with a newborn when I couldn't deal with myself? I hated the cries, and the early morning getting up to feed him. If you're wondering, yes, I was with his dad. We didn't get married until two years after his birth and his dad thought everything was fine with me because I was still walking around like I could handle the world. No one knew the difference and that's how my life went.

Depression is something you yourself don't know you suffer, because you are walking around and doing things like a regular functioning person. So when friends would come over to see the baby, I looked like an expert, but inside I was falling apart. That was my façade, not to show weakness or let anybody help me, because to me, I felt that if you helped me, you were only getting

The Mom In Me

in my way and not doing it right and that would only make me madder and I would start screaming, so the best thing to do was to keep my distance. Now, some days were good with the baby and I could take on the world but other days, I felt like throwing him out the window and I could actually visualize myself doing that. As time went on, he grew and so did my depression and the mania got worse because I felt like I was still a test dummy and not on my correct medication. Trying all those different medications drove me bananas. If I couldn't get settled in my mind, how was I supposed to take care of a child when my mind was racing? I could not focus on one thing and always seemed to be walking around like a raging bull waiting for someone to say the wrong word. This was not being a mom, but I did the best I could with what I had.

As my son grew older the battle didn't seem so tough, but he had issues when he was four years old. I would get calls from the daycare three to four days out of the week and guess what, that transformed me back into a dysfunctional raging bull, but I can say I never hurt my son, although he made parenting really hard for me since I wasn't completely settled in my own mind. I don't know if this was what God had planned for me, but I felt like he did. Out of all of this, God did speak to me and I wrote my very first book about my son and the trials that he went through, basically what we both went through, while he was four years old, but it also was exacerbated by the fact that his dad was deployed to Afghanistan. Go figure—I'm home alone again with a toddler and a brain that does what it wants to do. Tell me I didn't want to scream, but I never was homicidal or suicidal. Yes, through all of this I still was seeing my doctor and going to groups but I felt like they were not helping so I stopped.

For anybody who's reading this, I'm never advocating for you to stop taking your medication or stop going to group. As time passed my son continued to grow, of course, and every class he went to there were always issues with him, to the point I had to take him in to see his primary care doctor because we knew when he was four years old, he was diagnosed with having separation anxiety. So, I just figured that carried on into his older years, but who was I to make my own judgment when we both seemed like we were going through our own thing?

Brandon seemed to feed off me. The doctor told me that and I had to disclose to her what I had been living with for years and then the picture for him started to look a little bit clearer, but there was one thing I refused for them to do, and that was put a negative stigma on my son because he was diagnosed, like me, as bipolar. He does not exhibit any of those symptoms. He is just a boy, from the age of a toddler, who missed his dad and had a mom who did not know how to deal with it at the time.

My main concern now was getting to the root of what was bothering my son. I had a clue, and that was his dad being gone, so let's fix this. Tests were run to figure out what could be at the root of his acting out all the time and she came back with ADHD, and from there he began medication. At the time I was looking for anything that could ease my son's pain, and at first, believe it or not, the medication was working. Life as we knew it went on so all my issues went on the back burner, which was not the right thing to do because all it did was manifest and I forgot to take my medication for a while, and I was a ticking time bomb ready to blow, but at night when my son was asleep, I would cry, cry, cry because I felt so out of control and was second-guessing myself on how was I going to raise this son of mine without my husband being here to help. I was able to talk to my husband on a daily basis but guess what, he did not know I was almost wanting to fall off a cliff. That's the type of person I was; I would never let on that I needed help. I think that's the way I was built. When I'm in my mania I do things that are so careless that I do not care how it affects you, let alone me. I would go out and buy myself and my son things that we did not need; that was my way of pacifying him to be good, that was my bargaining tool because I did not want deal with all the drama he would cause in school. At home he would go in his room and I would go in my mine. We did not talk to each other like we should and now I look back and wish we had done that. He is just like me, anti-social, as people call it today.

At the time, trying to be a mom with everything I had going on, I did not teach my son people skills and all the things he would need to be a functioning part of society, but I can say he grew up to be a genius and I think that is one good part of having this wired-up brain that we have; he is a straight-A student, even with him acting out in elementary, middle and up until seventh grade. He made the decision to stop taking his medication and wanted to do things on his own, and I was very proud of him. Also, my son noticed that I had some things going on, because he is very intuitive and watches his surroundings and adjusts accordingly. That's another trait he got from me; we can adjust to everything we have going on because we want to be able to fix it ourselves. Believe me when I say I was glad when he got older and could do for himself on a certain level and then Dad came home but sometimes, I still felt that all of his being was with me because now he felt like I needed to be taken care of and I did not want to put what I had going on in my head on him, so I had to try to figure it out how I was going to fix this this issue after trying to raise him with a puzzled mind. That's a good word—I can call it a puzzled mind. You try to fix the pieces, and sometimes they get fixed, sometimes they don't.

Bran is a gamer now and in the 9th grade, with all As and two Bs. Yes, I'm a proud mom and his dad is ecstatic. I'm proud because he had a mom who didn't know right from left and was suffering with bipolar and anxiety and didn't fall off a cliff or jump into the sea. It was very hard at the beginning. I'm not going to tell anyone that it was not hard. There were days of nothing but crying and feeling like I didn't belong and asking myself how I was going to raise a son; there was so much more I was thinking about. My only fault is that I had really good friends and I didn't rely on them for fear of being judged and them thinking they could raise my son better than I could or telling me how I should do this or that and do it this way, because you see, if you tell me to do something I get really upset and start cursing you out because I do not want to hear it. It was just better that I did not tell them anything at all.

When I wrote the book *Cryin' Out*, my friends said, "I did not know you went through all of that and why did you not call us? We would have been there." In my head I was saying, *Ok, let's move on*. You are probably wondering where my hubby was. He was there once he got back from deployment so a lot of things Bran has learned came from him, but to this day Bran is still like me. We'd rather be alone in a room by ourselves, never to be disturbed again. I made it through this difficult time because even though I was sick, I constantly talked to God about what I was feeling and yes,

The Mom In Me

I asked Him, *Why me?* It was the fight and determination in me that got me through this because I did not want my son to see me suffer so I pulled myself back up and went back to my doctor and finally got on medication that is working for me, but the downside is, it's only taken at night and the anxiety had gotten so bad I had to be provided medication during the day to help. Irritation is not a diagnosis, but I developed that too.

So you see, I'm dealing with a lot and need to be very calm. I'm back in therapy groups that are helping but I still feel like a yo-yo sometimes. But I have determination to make it and to not let my son see me fail—that's my dream and goal: to make it and be happy for him or shall I say, continue to be and be there for him.

This journey has not been easy by any means, but I'm going to continue to do what I have to so my diagnosis won't get me down and keep me down because I have a lot to live for and yes, that's my son. Now, one thing I must say: I am an animal person and I have cats and a chihuahua and they have been a comforting blanket to me as well, so when people say animals are good therapy, they are telling the truth. I'm making it through this milestone now with the help of my son, who is now 15. It's almost like the roles have reversed but he is a very well-rounded young man and I'm very proud of him and I have to say so myself because it could have been worse.

Even though I went through the worst, I still was able to raise him to be a very respectable young man. How did I do all of this living with bipolar and the other illnesses? As I said before, it was not easy because it's like my brain is racing and I'm fighting with myself and wanting to just lie in bed all day. Have you ever felt that feeling of hopelessness, worthlessness, loss of energy? All that is a terrible feeling; it feels like your body has shut down but when you have responsibilities you push and push to do what you must. Some days I just go off to myself and have a ME moment because it is needed. Sometimes, darn it, it almost feels like all the time but I cannot fall into that pattern. I have to be able to elicit help from friends. Don't do like I did, and refuse to ask for help. Let me tell you, depression isn't always dark rooms and crying endlessly. Sometimes it's getting up, going to work and smiling and laughing all day and then coming home to sit quietly, doing little to nothing until it's time to go to bed. I also want to say do not be afraid to talk about your diagnosis of mental health issues, because you need that help from other people and professionals; if not, you manifest things in your head that are not there, and that can lead you to thinking of suicide because you feel that you have a lot to do, feel hopeless, like no one cares about you, or worthless, and these feelings weigh heavy on a person like me who has depression. So please, take it from me and don't think about what others perceive about you, just think about yourself and your family and continue to get help and talk; it's just that simple. I am in group now, and some days I do not want to go because I'm so low in the dumps but that's ok, I get right back up the next day and start over.

Depression and Bipolar disorder: I have the diagnosis, but just like my diagnosis of diabetes, I'm living WITH it not FOR it.

Here are just a few tips that have helped me through when I thought the world was closing in around me. Number one was one that I was always scared to do but now it has become not easier, but a lot less threatening to me.

1. Talking to others
2. Exercise
3. Reduce stress
4. Journaling
5. Meditate
6. Listening to music

DO NOT ISOLATE YOURSELF!!

Get up, get out, and let's talk about it!! We are here for each other. We can't battle this alone.

"Mother's love is peace.
It need not be acquired,
it need not be deserved."

– Erich Fromm

Rev. LaShonda Durden is an Educator, Liberator, and Advocate, passionate about helping females manifest a healthy future. She creates virtual and in-person sacred spaces for females to heal from trauma. LaShonda is a truth-teller: teaching Love, Mercy, Grace, Sacrifice, and Redemption without sounding "preachy or pushy". She has spoken in the US, Jamaica, Prague, Turkey, and Canada. Her target audience is females seeking healthier life transitions.

Understanding the generational effects of internal and external imbalances, she founded The Infusion, Inc. ten years ago to break cycles by making connections. She launched A Different Mom (Life Group) to help females Master Mommyhood.

LaShonda graduated from Georgia State University with a BA in Sociology and an M.Div. from Columbia Theological Seminary. She lives with her family in Metro Atlanta.

Topics of expertise:
Living Better to Die Well   Sacred Sexuality
When Wellness Looks Different   Career Development
Safe Housing

Connect: www.theinfusionconnects.org
theinfusion7@gmail.com
adifferentmom@gmail.com

THROWING THE BABY OUT WITH THE BATH WATER – REIMAGINING REST

LASHONDA DURDEN

It was 2005. I survived becoming an adult in the 1990s while living in Atlanta, Georgia. It was the best of times. I was beginning an internship to complete my Master of Divinity degree (it was earned). So many things were wrapping up in my life, and I was excited at the opportunity to really go wherever and do whatever I wanted in service to the Most High and my community. I was a trained chaplain specializing in hospice, bereavement, and grief. I enjoyed dream interpretation workshops that allowed us to discuss and process our personal dream content. Now that I think about it...I was able to rest enough to remember my dreams...like I said, it was the best of times. I was being pushed mentally and spiritually and I loved it! I participated in small group sessions and individual therapy to ensure I was dealing with all my stuff so as to not project it onto my coworkers, patients, or their loved ones. The debates, the raw emotions, the support, the love, the pain, the release of so much trauma—it didn't feel good then but it ended well. I made the choice to confront my demons, confront the people, confront the places, confront the bipolar challenges, confront the lies, confront all that I had imagined into reality. The result felt like freedom. It was freedom...nothing stopping me from whatever the next level of soaring looked like for me. I graduated from seminary feeling "ready"—ready to conquer the world, ready to go and be the chaplain I was called to be.

Everything was on par to be amazing...I had a third-floor apartment with a view above the tree line. The wind blew daily through my sheer curtains. I could see the sun and the moon in their full glory from my bed. I was employed, productive, and like I said, ready.

I remember the day all that began to change. I was having what I thought was a great chat with my best friend since kindergarten. She had become a full-time stay-at-home mom since giving birth to her now two-year-old. She was a teacher and decided that her gifts would be best used in her home. Good for her. As she shared about trying to navigate sleep, hair, food, and marriage, I shared about sleeping. I shared about napping after work, sleeping late on the weekends, napping after shopping, napping after brunch, napping after dinner or whenever I felt like napping. I shared my late-night Wal-Mart runs just to go; my midnight Taco Bell runs just because I wanted Mexican pizza (no beans, extra meat). She shared about poop and mom life. I was content with that not being my life. As we continued sharing, she said, "Shonnie, you need a baby." "No the fuck I don't!!! Why would you even put something like that in the atmosphere? I am good. Just because that is your life, I am enjoying mine...and how selfish of you to even put that out there." I don't remember what she said in response but I am pretty sure she said, "OK. But you do."

I was so upset with her because I had been allowing her to speak LIFE into my life for 25 years (at that time). She was my cheerleader. I could call her anytime and get a one-person pep rally with no warning. We rolled like that, supporting each other through it all. But what was this nonsense being spewed out of her mouth? How could she be hating on my career and life so much? That's what I wanted to believe but I knew deep down this chick always only had my best interest at heart. But damn, I didn't want a baby right then; I was about to buy a convertible Toyota Solara, white with a beige leather top. That was my plan and I was sticking to it.

Like I said earlier, I was wrapping up my degree and found myself confronting the last of my childhood demons...rape. I successfully offered my truth to my family and ended up vomiting and sick from the release of all that toxicity. Well, maybe that was part of it, because after a few days of not really feeling like myself I learned I was pregnant.

This Bitch... was all I could think as I looked at the pregnancy test results. *How could she curse me like this at this time in my life?* That was my initial reaction but I knew it had nothing to do with her except the Most High had allowed her to warn me if I chose to listen.

I gave birth to a little girl who looked exactly like my mother and my head began to spin...*I have given birth to my mother.* So many thoughts flooded my brain as I held this little angel for the first time. I was so glad she was finally out of me. I was glad I would be able to sleep on my stomach, or back, or BED again. I had pretty much used the La-Z-Boy recliner as my primary mode of "rest" since my daughter thought that when I stopped moving for the night that was her cue to begin doing whatever she was doing that did not include being still...this went on for the last five months of my pregnancy. So relief was an understatement when she was out! Little did I know sleep was farther from me now than EVER.

We brought this bundle home, cared for her, nurtured her, loved her, fed her, walked her, burped her. I went for my follow-up and everything was good. NOPE, I wasn't pregnant again and hadn't even had sex. My dad and I decided to take this little baby to Barbados (his homeland) at the ripe age of three months. When my husband picked us up from the airport we went to Wendy's and I ordered a bacon double cheeseburger. My first thought was, *Ewww...I don't even eat pork.* Then the unthinkable happened. I actually ate it and I knew immediately that my body had been invaded AGAIN!

My internal dialogue was interesting: *I cannot believe this. Yeah, how you gonna be pregnant again and this baby is just three months? Well, you know you're most fertile after giving birth. How am I gonna carry another baby so quick, when my body isn't even healed? I am not ready. Well, you must be ready 'cause you're pregnant.* And there we had it...I was pregnant again and if I wasn't ready, I wouldn't be pregnant. So ok, here we go AGAIN.

Baby girl would not sleep. Her brother was born a year and a day after her birthday. One year and one day. Fifteen months with no real rest.

I had transitioned from 150% sleep to 50% or less in the twinkling of an eye. We would feed, bathe, pray, and tuck in this angel and go to the next task. Regardless of the schedule, this baby would not stay asleep...sugar, worms, eczema, allergies, being nosy, whatever—I don't know. All I knew was sleep and rest had left the building and I was past tired. I was tired of not sleeping, tired of trying to figure out what was out of balance that our child couldn't sleep, tired of breastfeeding but I knew the importance. I had lost too much weight because my son had his grandfather's stomach and metabolism...so he ate and was healthy and thriving and sucking the life out of me, literally.

Detached

My son was so handsome and smart. Even before he arrived, I asked him to please wait until after his sister's first birthday before he made his grand entrance into the world. He was so kind as to grant my request to wait until the day after her birthday to let me know he was ready by breaking my water at 3 AM. We had decided to breast feed again. My husband called me the milk machine and that is what I felt like: a freaking cow. If I wasn't changing a baby, I was feeding a baby, if I wasn't feeding a baby, I was trying to get a nap, which almost never happened or if it did, I don't remember.

The pain of postpartum depression is indescribable...the numbness from sleep deprivation is crippling.

I held my baby in my arms with tears in my eyes and thought I could throw this child against this wall and this would be over… I could get some sleep...my body could rest...I could actually get some sleep. In retrospect, I didn't think about the fact that I would be in jail after that point or maybe I knew that I could plead insanity because I had truly lost my mind to even consider throwing a baby into the wall and not just any baby... my baby. I don't know if this was rock bottom for me because I contemplated numerous methods to end my suffering by ending their lives, but it definitely made me know something had to give.

My mom always said to tell her before I did anything I would regret...she told me to tell her if it was really too much and she would take the children and help me so I could rest. She had experienced two babies two years apart, which is different but not really. I was ready to come clean and tell her, "Ma, I really am struggling. I am having crazy thoughts. You told me to tell you, and at this point I am really scaring myself because I am so tired, I can't think." I had my words all ready to go.

Instead of me telling her I was dying, literally, she began sharing that she found a lump in her breast along her bra line where "people don't get cancer" but this lump was hard, sore, and felt like it was trying to travel deeper inside her body. She talked about going to the doctor and demanding x-rays for months (I had completely lost track of all time at this point). All I knew for sure was I was getting no rest, she kept talking about doctor's appointments, and she was relentless. After several months she called to say she was scheduled for a biopsy that ended up coming back positive. I sat and reflected: *What do you mean you have cancer? You are the cleanest and healthiest woman I know. What about these children? I need help! I need you, Ma!*

She ended up having a double mastectomy and lumpectomy, which pretty much meant she was 100% unavailable. Shit. Ok...so much for my plan to tell her I was dying because she was for real for real. This was the hardest thing I have ever dealt with because I wanted to be there with her all the time, I wanted her to know I was there, but the reality was I had two little babies, both under three. My husband helped with the babies so much to allow me to help her, but it never felt like I was doing enough for her. Don't get me wrong; she did not lack support from family and friends, but I wanted to be there so much more. I just couldn't. She couldn't hold and hug her grandbabies and that sucked the most because that's what grandbabies are for. Nevertheless, my sleeplessness continued because now I worried for my daughter, my mother, myself. I worried for my husband and son. I worried if I would be like the chicks on *Snapped* and really just lose it. I could see that happening despite my prayers and efforts to stay positive and healthy.

It's gonna take a long time to heal (Accidents happen)

Heading to my grandmother's house I was rear-ended and my car was pushed into another car. I was wearing my seatbelt but my head hit the steering wheel. My physician warned my husband, "It's gonna take her a long time to heal from this injury. It is equivalent to a hockey player's head trauma." Yeah, judging from the pain in my body and the imbalance in my energy levels I knew this was bad... really bad. I knew that time and a lot of focused energy would heal me but for real, how was I gonna do this? I needed rest. I had two babies under three, my mother had just been diagnosed with breast cancer, I had just lost my job, and now my brain was rattled.

The struggle was real. I had girlfriends who had also just given birth around the time I did and we were all in the trenches together.

Every woman was dealing with her own level of sleep deprivation, depression, accidents, marriage, divorce, careers, aging parents, college degrees, certifications, and everything under the sun.

It got bad, y'all. Especially bonding with my son…I had nothing to give him, other than the milk he was sucking out of me. I adored him but something was missing. I knew it was me, I knew it was my energy, and I had no idea how to fix it. I had no one to reach out to and I felt so alone. My husband took up so much of the slack because he saw daily, I was done. I slept but it was more like a coma than sleep. I did not rest because my spirit was suffering…worrying…drained. I recall him handing me our son when it was feeding time; I would feed him and take him right back to his father. This went on for months. We had finally gotten some resolutions in our daughter's health situation and I exhaled. My husband brought me the baby boy, I fed him and got up to take him back to his father as was the routine, but this time this little baby (less than six months) wrapped his little arm around my neck as if to say, "Please Mommy, just hold me for a little while. I have been so patient, my sister is sleeping now, and I just want to lie with you; please don't take me back yet"…and I cried. I told my baby boy how much I loved him, and how grateful I was that he was mine, how amazing he was and that I would always be aware of his feelings. I sat back down and held him (although he was really holding me at that point). We sat there in the dark and allowed the bond that he deserved from birth to form, and I cried because I was so thankful for such an understanding being choosing me. I knew that this baby was special… always so considerate, always kind, always compassionate, just like his father.

Reattached – Realizing (again) that the choices I make are mine to deal with has been an ongoing growing edge for me

Mom survived and thrives as I write this chapter, and we are thankful. The children, now 13 and 14, are my angels and yeah, my BFF was right; I needed a baby. They have helped me to see myself more clearly. They are truly sponges, and mirrors. They make me laugh at our similarities and our differences. They make me cry when I think of how they are changing the world with their strength, their insight, their genuine love for truth, their quest for knowledge. They make me shake my head when they refuse to be muted, ignored or silenced because though I still struggle with my tone sometimes, I have instilled in them how they can control any situation with respect and kindness. They teach me so much.

Here are a few affirmations I embraced to help remind myself of how I needed to implement changes in my own life to better love others.

I will not give all the decision-making power to the other person and I will trust myself more.

I will be responsible for my own emotional/ physical/ mental/ spiritual health and not depend on others for my happiness and vice versa.

I now acknowledge my sacred sexuality and I accept it. I don't know what that means in the long run but we will see. I have a baby to deliver and to raise. Regardless of who may or may not be in the picture, I will do a wonderful job of loving my child and trying desperately not to repeat the mistakes of the past while remembering all of the things my parents got right.

I am going to find a nurturing community of faith where I am comfortable.

I am seriously considering how to more faithfully honor my gifts.

I will try not to begin any new relationships until I am really able to emotionally commit with no strings attached.

I am going to make a conscious effort to depend on the people who are walking with me, even if I have to ask, "How do you think you can help me in this?"

I am going to join a health facility.

I am going to listen to my dreams and trust them to direct me.

I am going to listen to and trust my own voice.

I am going to let myself feel pain, knowing that if I can't feel pain, I can't feel any other emotion. Pain won't kill me—truth-telling, if done the right way and out of love, won't kill the other person.

Mommy, Ma, Mom 10/26/2012

That's what they call me all day and all night long:

Mommy, Ma, Mom.

I can't even go to the bathroom without somebody calling me:

Mama, what you dooooing?

Mama, can I have some ice cream? some pizza? some chicken nuggets? some juice? some water? some candy?

Ma, can I come in?

Mommy, how long are you going to be in there?

Well, I will just sit here and wait for you to come out…

Mommy, Ma, Mom—that's what they call me.

Maybe I could run away to a faraway place like a beach with sand

and maybe I could lie down… get some rest in the sand

and sink into the ground. Maybe I could become the sand

and no one can find me to say:

Mommy, I need…

Mommy, I want…

Mommy where is…

Mommy, can you please buy me…

show me…

The Mom In Me

get me...

take me...

bring me...

fix my...

Mom, he...

or she...

Mom, I...

Mommy, you don't...

Mommy, you never...

Mommy, you won't...

Maybe I could round up all the other mothers
and they could all go away with me.

Moms and any others who may be reading this: I beg you to please, please allow yourself a network of safe people or one person. I know for those of us who have experienced early childhood trauma that may be much easier said than done. I can only empathize with my global family and friends who are suffering from SEVERE sleep deprivation with no end in sight. Please pray that you feel comfortable with someone, anyone who is safe, willing, and able to care for your child or children while you practice a little or a lot of self-care. For a person who has never experienced sleep deprivation, it is impossible to imagine what we go through, and that is ok. It may not be for you to understand. You may be just the person to help out because you get a full eight or more. Moms, please be open to help, even if it doesn't come in the manner you expect.

ABOUT THE VISIONARY AUTHOR

Kimmoly K. LaBoo is a Published Author, International Speaker and Certified Master Life Coach. She is at the helm of LaBoo Publishing Enterprise, as CEO and founder. She is a highly respected change agent in her community and around the world.

Her award-winning company was created for the independent self-publisher. Kimmoly enjoys providing expert guidance and unlimited support to her clients, helping them recognize their brilliance, sharing their stories with the world, as writers.

She has dedicated her life to serving girls and women through mentoring, and coaching. Her compassionate coaching style, challenges clients to embrace change and show up confidently, using their unique gifts and talents to impact and serve others.

She was recently named among the Top 25 Women in Business by Courageous Woman magazine. She has appeared on Think Tech Hawaii, WPB Networks, Heaven 600, ABC2News, FOX5 News, and has graced many stages speaking and training to include, Department of Veterans Affairs, Blacks in Government National Training Conference, and Coppin State University.

Kimmoly is the mother of two amazing sons and currently resides in Baltimore, Maryland.

Contact Information:
www.laboopublishing.com
staff@laboopubishing.com

ALSO BY KIMMOLY K. LABOO

The Mom in Me
Stories and Practical Advice from Moms
Who have Survived Parenting

I've heard it said that being a mom is like watching your heart walk around outside of your body. No matter how protective we are there are somethings guaranteed to be out of our control. Yet, as mothers, we put on our brave faces and we set out to conquer and overcome whatever challenges motherhood throws our way.

Twenty-one valiant moms have collaborated to share how they have pushed through and survived seemingly insurmountable obstacles. Being a mom isn't about being perfect. I promise you, there is no perfect mom on this earth. What you will see in the pages of this book is the strength, determination, and courage of these incredible mom's, told through the experiences they have endured along one of the most daring journeys we as women can ever attempt – Motherhood.

Paperback, 242 pages, ISBN 978-1735112664

Set Apart and Chosen
God uses ordinary women to do extraordinary things

God never reveals His entire plan for our lives. If He did, we would likely be overwhelmed and immediately abort the plan out of fear. Instead, He carefully weaves His plans and our choices together for good. Set Apart and Chosen, God uses ordinary women to do extraordinary things is the intricate look into the lives of twenty extraordinary women who have overcome great odds to walk fully in the gift God has given them. It is said that hindsight is 20/20. We invite you into our lives in hopes that you will gain strength, clarity, courage, and boldness, to step out on faith, claiming everything that God has purposed for your life. The women in this book have discovered, even though they didn't understand their trials while amidst them, God has now given them great revelation about their gifts and how they are to use what they have overcome to bless the lives of others. Maybe you are in a season of your life where you can't see your way forward. We invite you to share in our victories, realizing God shows no partiality. If He was gracious enough to see us through, He can and will do it for you.

Paperback, 204 pages, ISBN 978-1732810457

A Threefold Cord Broken
What happens when Christian marriages fail

A Threefold Cord Broken is an honest, heartfelt depiction of the journey seven courageous Christian women experienced during the challenge of divorce. Each gives a glimpse into their marriage, what went wrong, how they navigated the process as a Christian, how they overcame, the lessons learned, and where they are now. The stories shared will give insight, hope, courage, and healing to others. It will enlighten those who think God has abandoned them or will somehow continually punish them for their choice to divorce. Encouraging, confirming, and reminding women that God may hate divorce, but He will never hate them. A valuable resource for those who are engaged, married, separated, or divorced.

Paperback, 78 pages, ISBN 978-1981529605

The Black Father Perspective
What we want America to know

Black fathers play a pivotal role in the lives of our black children. According to the 2011 U.S. Census, nearly 2 in 3 (64%) African American children live in father-absent homes. However, we know all fathers are not absent. Society would have us to believe that black fathers are either in jail, or on drugs and are no good to the community. The Black Father Perspective is a collaboration of men who have come together to give voice to a population that is often overlooked and underappreciated. It is time to change the narrative. It is time to shift the agenda. Ten black fathers share their view on legacy, marriage, divorce, single parenting, teenage parenting, incarceration, child support and so much more. Reading this book will give you a new perspective of Black Fathers in America. This is what they want you to know.

Paperback, 140 pages, ISBN 978-1735112602

www.ingramcontent.com/pod-product-compliance
Lightning Source LLC
Chambersburg PA
CBHW070517100426
42743CB00010B/1851